GRIPPED BY THE GREATNESS

GOD

OF

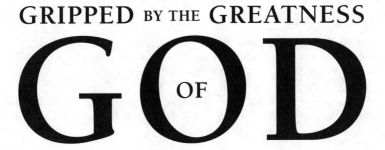

GRIPPED BY THE GREATNESS

GOD
OF

JAMES MACDONALD

MOODY PUBLISHERS
CHICAGO

All Scripture quotations, unless otherwise indicated, are taken from the *New American Standard Bible*®, © Copyright The Lockman Foundation 1960, 1962, 1963, 1968, 1971, 1972, 1973, 1975, 1977, 1995. Used by permission.

Scripture quotations marked ESV are taken from *The Holy Bible, English Standard Version*. Copyright © 2000,2001 by Crossway Bibles, a division of Good News Publishers. Used by permission. All rights reserved.

Scripture quotations marked NKJV are taken from the *New King James Version*. Copyright © 1982 by Thomas Nelson, Inc. Used by permission. All rights reserved.

Scripture quotations marked KJV are taken from the King James Version.

Library of Congress Cataloging-in-Publication Data

MacDonald, James, 1960-
   Gripped by the greatness of God / James MacDonald.
      p. cm.
   Includes bibliographical references.
   ISBN-13: 978-0-8024-4778-4
    1. God. 2. Spirituality. 3. Christian life. I. Title.

BT103.M235 2005
231—dc22

                                                            2005010074

ISBN: 0-8024-4778-3
ISBN-13: 978-0-8024-4778-4

CLOTH ISBN: 0-8024-4779-1
CLOTH ISBN-13: 978-0-8024-4779-1

1 3 5 7 9 10 8 6 4 2

Printed in the United States of America

To Luke,
Landon,
and Abby

Seeing the grip of our Creator
so soon and so obvious
in each of your lives
is our deepest gratitude
and our highest praise!

We "**have no greater joy than this,**
to hear of [our] **children walking in the truth.**"
3 John 4

CONTENTS

ACKNOWLEDGMENTS

IT'S THE LONGING of every human heart, even before we know what it is or how to fill it: To be gripped by the reality of who this awesome God really is. Again and again during some of the busiest days our lives have seen, I have reluctantly undertaken the role of author only to personally—and immensely—benefit as I have felt His grip afresh. God is faithful to Himself and to His Word, and we who place ourselves in the flow of that unceasing work are the continual benefactors. Though these messages were first preached several years ago, the timeless nature of God's Word has refreshed these truths in my heart as they have gone from oral to written format.

That process involves a number of people worthy of my sincerest thanks. Rosa Sabatino, who listens to each message and carefully types the transcript. Barb Peil, who creates a rough draft of each chapter, eliminating the obvious and adding the essential. You are everything a writing partner should be and more. Kathy Elliott, my personal assistant of sixteen years, has worked as usual, greasing the wheels and making sure it all comes together.

Acknowledgments

Deepest thanks to the people of Harvest Bible Chapel, who embrace our vision for a lifetime of ministry together with the faith and forbearance that strengthens true commitment. To my precious wife, Kathy, who has pushed and prodded, prayed and provided, I give my special thanks. After twenty-two years, your love undiminished brings joy unimagined.

Most of all, thanks are due to our great God and Savior Jesus Christ, who gripped this lost soul so long ago and by His grace has never let go.

READ THIS FIRST!

LAME, LAME, LAME.

Sad but true; that is the way I would describe most Sunday services in the country church I attended as a child. All that was alive in the Word of God had been smothered by a rules-oriented religion that had degenerated into a form-without-function faith. A dead orthodoxy that rang the bell of right doctrine but too often left the heart cold and listless. Tragically, many believers would call it "the only church I have ever known." I would call it "church without God."

Please don't get me wrong. I'm certain my church leaders loved Christ with their minds. They faithfully studied, even memorized, huge sections of Scripture. Beyond that, I am confident they tried to live in obedience to God's Word. But looking back it seems we most often missed the part God loves the most . . . the *heart* part (1 Samuel 12:24).

Jesus warned of honoring God with our lips while our hearts are far from Him (Matthew 15:8). He was quoting Scripture—the prophet

Isaiah circa 740 B.C.—so obviously this is not a new problem. This kind of ritual religion may *think* and sometimes even *act* biblically— in a military sort of way—but it doesn't prompt the followers of Jesus to *feel* what they should be feeling. You might label it apathetic, formulaic, even perfunctory. I just call it lame.

By the time I became a pastor, I was determined that I would never tolerate that kind of indifference in my own heart again.

It all changed for me the first time I was gripped by the greatness of God. I was sixteen years old, attending a camp in upstate New York. I met believers who loved God with obvious zeal and simple, genuine faith. I sang songs that felt fresh and alive with sincere adoration, and, most of all, I heard preaching that was passionate about God Himself rather than simply an extrabiblical code of conduct.

Yes, there on the shores of Schroon Lake, New York, in the heart of the Adirondack Mountains, I was gripped by the greatness of God. I was gladly captured at the core of my being. I felt incredible! Phenomenal! Totally immersed in a heaving sea of love and commitment to my Creator.

When was the last time you were gripped by the greatness of God?

When I got home from camp, all I could say to my parents was, "Mom and Dad, I think I found God." Although my faith had its struggles for a couple more years, I knew deep inside that I was truly changed. Since that summer in 1976 the Lord has taken and shaken me many times, and I would not return to the faith I had before.

Never again would I be content executing religious obligation as a substitute for the touch of God's greatness upon my heart.

Key question: When did God last take you to the mat with the reality of who He is, and with the nearness of eternity and the triviality of this life by comparison? I'm asking you straight up—when was the last time you were gripped?

My guess is that one reason you picked up this book is because you long to feel that wonder again. When was the last time you let God get a grip on your heart? No vague answers to this question, OK? Get specific. What year? What month? How long has it been? This isn't the kind of thing you can forget. Has it *ever* happened? Please, no guilt here. There was a time in my life when my honest answer would have been, no!

But there is hope. A couple of years ago I longed to see God grip the hearts of folks in our church. I loved them too much to see them live one more day apart from the grasp of God upon them. To this end, I chose to teach what I believe are the most gripping passages in Scripture. In my preparation of those messages, I was shaken afresh by God's awesome, holy, sovereign character. And now I'm grateful for the privilege of sharing these truths with you.

Buckle your seat belt, because you're in for the ride of your life. (Yeah, really!) God is not safe, and He will not be squeezed into some neat, respectable Sunday discussion. God in a box—with a little packet of hot sauce and a toy surprise. No. To know God at all is to watch Him explode any box we put Him in with His terror, majesty, and indescribable wonder. God says, "Get Me out of the box. Know Me as I am—the One who was and is and is to come [Revelation 1:8]. Eternal. Holy. Awesome. Sovereign. Lord of all."

God invites us to be gripped by His greatness. Shaken to the core of our being at the realization of what He freely offers. The King of creation welcomes us into His throne room for just a glimpse of His glory, and we fall on our faces.

Are you scared? Are you wondering if I am talking about some weird, way-out-there, flesh-manufactured strangeness? I'm not. I think I understand why people do a lot of bizarre things to get their piece of God. I'm not surprised when folks drive across the country or fly across the world to be part of such supposed supernatural happenings. (As if God would make someone He loves bark like a dog!?) The counterfeit is present because the reality beckons so strongly. Each of us longs not just to know God, but to experience Him.

But we must not let our zeal for God lead us away from the way He revealed Himself to us—through Scripture. Genuine encounters with God must be measured against and can never stray from the anchor of God's Word. Don't settle for cheap substitutes! Jesus said, **"God is spirit, and those who worship Him must worship in spirit and truth"** (John 4:24).

The kind of gripping experience I'm talking about has nothing to do with unbiblical extravagance. I'm talking about what Paul felt on the Damascus road, and John in his revelatory vision of things to come. And the burning awesomeness that Moses experienced as he stood by a bush or hid in the cleft of the rock. I have in mind what Samuel must have sensed as he spoke the transforming words, **"Speak, LORD, for Your servant is listening"** (1 Samuel 3:9).

Some will argue that the dramatic encounters of the Bible are not essential for us today because we have the Scripture in our hands and the Holy Spirit in our hearts. But don't let those facts allow you to settle for a faith from the shoulders up.

That kind of experience only happens when God penetrates our hearts through the truth of His Word and drives the indifference and complacency from our souls.

EXPERIENCING GOD IN THE HIGHEST PEAKS OF SCRIPTURE

For me, those kinds of clear, gripping encounters happen most when I am scaling the highest peaks of Scripture. The *highest*—not necessarily the deepest or most complicated sections. Not the toughest passages to understand, but the places where God says irrefutably, "Look here! It's Me, and I am like . . . !" Many of those peaks are in the Old Testament book of Isaiah— so that's where we are headed.

> We don't long for the dramatic —we long for the unmistakable, the genuine unveiling of the glory of God.

Isaiah is considered to be the prince of all prophets. He ministered without compromise in a day of moral decline and preached the holiness of God during the reign of four kings. From Isaiah's lips poured forth dignified oratory like the world had never heard. Hebrew scholars will tell you his language is the most eloquent in all of the Old Testament.

Even Isaiah's personal testimony spoke of courage and faith. While Jonah ran, Jeremiah wept, and Habakkuk cried, "How long?" Isaiah stood and proclaimed the righteous majesty of God and the coming Messiah. He delivered our most treasured prophecies concerning Christ—740 years before the Savior was even born.

Ever wonder how Isaiah became such a pure, powerful, and

prophetic spokesman for God? I'll tell you how. On the day that God called him into ministry, He gave him an unparalleled, unprecedented, private tour of His heavenly throne room. And Isaiah was changed forever by what he saw. This same vision is one that we desperately, desperately need in the church today. Such a view of God rocks your world and turns your faith upside down . . . but wow, right side up.

So if you're weary to death of laboring under an almost ceremonial remembrance of God and a distant reminiscence of when your faith was vibrant, if you're ready and willing to engage in a *current* experience with God, to be gripped afresh by the Father, the Creator, the Judge, the King, . . . please return your seats to the upright position and stow all carry-on baggage under the seat in front of you. . . .

A WORD ABOUT OUR FORMAT

Before we begin, I think a brief explanation of the format ahead will prove helpful. No doubt His grip upon you will be firmer and fuller if you enter into these added features with your whole heart.

Before Reading the Chapter

Read the listed passage in Isaiah that precedes each chapter or, better yet, read that section in your own Bible. Get an overall picture of what Isaiah is saying before you begin our detailed study together. Read the passage in context and you'll get more out of it. Mark up the Bible section by underlining or circling important words or adding margin comments—it'll help you engage in what's important and will serve as a reminder of what you learned when you read it again later on. *Note:* All that I am going to share comes from God's holy Word, the Bible. Consider its words with immense reverence and respect. God is speaking; let your heart be filled with faith as you focus on His words, and God Himself promises it will accomplish His purpose in you (Isaiah 55:11).

As You Read Each Chapter

Note that a "Snapshot Summary" appears before the title of each chapter. Like aiming a gun at a target, this summary will help you scope into the main theme of the chapter. I know these kinds of things really help me when I read.

Take a moment to read the sidebar: "Get a Grip on God's Greatness." Each chapter's sidebar will introduce you to one of God's names and how that relates to the attribute discussed in that chapter. God wants you to call Him by name. This section will help you learn new names for God that can amplify the message of His greatness.

Be sure to read carefully: "It Happened to Me." In writing, I try to answer the questions I find myself asking when I am reading a book. (Yes, authors also read!) Often as I read the insights of others, I find myself wondering, *Is this happening in your life?* A long time ago I heard someone say, "You can't teach what you don't know, and you can't lead where you don't go." I would not waste your time with pious platitudes that have never made it into my personal experience. To avoid that danger, in each chapter I am including a personal account of being gripped by God's greatness—an encounter with God that has shaken my experience and shaped my own faith. My goal in sharing so personally with you is that you will know what to look for in your own experience and be confident that it *can* happen to you.

And the best part . . .

After Reading the Chapter

"Make It Personal" provides three to five practical application steps you can take based on the chapter's teaching points. Usually they will include something to do, something to think about, and something to commit to God. Don't just read them and think, *Hmm . . . that's nice.* Go ahead and take action! Transformation takes engagement. If you want proof of that, just review James 1:22–24. In God's eyes, it's the person who does what the Word says who gets blessed; everyone else is sort of wasting his time. So let's put what we're learning into practice. And finally . . .

The Closing Prayer

Never close the chapter without praying about what you've read. The prayer I've written is just a place to start. Don't let my words limit what you want to say to God. Tell Him how you desire His truth to grip your heart. Lean into application in a fresh way each time. Be open to His Spirit hammering away at stuff in your life that doesn't belong there and building on the good things He has already done in your heart. Kneeling down, folding your hands, and bowing your head, praying out loud—each of these are actions in the physical realm that enhance our capacity to enter the spiritual realm through prayer. If you "get into it," you will get much more out of it.

Get ready to be stunned by His glory—gripped by almighty God. Shaken in a way that is greater than any Richter scale can measure. *This* is the God who owns the universe. *This* is the God Isaiah saw **"sitting on a throne, lofty and exalted, with the train of His robe filling the temple"** (6:1).

Remember, this is just where it starts, or starts again. We will spend the rest of our lives and into eternity captured by the most glorious, life-rattling, astounding discovery a human being can make. To be gripped, truly gripped by the greatness of God. It's never going to end.

So let's get started.

Now, your first assignment: Pray and turn the page.

Great God,

Lord of the Universe and Lover of my soul—I come to this study feeling a bit nervous and curious at what I will discover about You. But I come. I come because I cannot stay away. I come in humility and anticipation of a fresh beginning with You. I mean that I really want to know You as You are. I'm not satisfied to follow man's dusty, diluted version of You. I want the real thing. All of You.

So here is all of me. Teach me; guide me in Your truth. Grip my heart with Your greatness so I am never the same. I invite Your Spirit to meet me in these pages. Help me to **"open my eyes, that I may behold wonderful things from Your Law"** (Psalm 119:18).

Give me strength for the climb.

In Your holy name I pray.

—*Amen.*

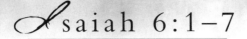

In the year of King Uzziah's death I saw the Lord sitting on a throne, lofty and exalted, with the train of His robe filling the temple. Seraphim stood above Him, each having six wings: with two he covered his face, and with two he covered his feet, and with two he flew. And one called out to another and said,

> "Holy, Holy, Holy, is the LORD of hosts,
> The whole earth is full of His glory."

And the foundations of the thresholds trembled at the voice of him who called out, while the temple was filling with smoke. Then I said,

> "Woe is me, for I am ruined!
> Because I am a man of unclean lips,
> And I live among a people of unclean lips;
> For my eyes have seen the King, the LORD of hosts."

Then one of the seraphim flew to me with a burning coal in his hand, which he had taken from the altar with tongs. He touched my mouth with it and said, "Behold, this has touched your lips; and your iniquity is taken away and your sin is forgiven."

God's holiness separates us from Him

and yet compels us to be like Him.

Chapter One

GRIPPED
by the
HOLINESS
of GOD

Isaiah 6:1–7

I AM DEEPLY CONVICTED in my heart that this is one of the most important studies you have ever undertaken. Isaiah has a message about God that, if we let it take us and shake us, we will never be the same. A joy-producing, fulfillment-enhancing, life-exhilarating change. The kind of change you would expect when you are gripped by the Creator and Designer of your own soul.

Ready—here we go.

Every journey begins with the first step. This first step in climbing God's great mountain means we walk in Isaiah's footsteps and see what Isaiah saw—the immense, indescribable, incomprehensible holiness of God. Maybe you're thinking, *Whoa, can't we start with His love or mercy or something more friendly, and then sort of work our way up to holiness?* The answer is no. We don't get to choose where we start—God is in charge of that. So we'll start where God started with Isaiah—with His holiness.

Holiness. What image does that conjure up in your mind? My

earliest image of holiness is standing in a little country Baptist church. I was maybe five years old, staring straight ahead with my brothers, all stiff and stale, my suit and tie choking the life out of me. In the same row were my father, grandfather, and great-grandfather, all gripping the pew in front of them till their knuckles turned white. They sang at the top of their lungs, a medieval organ backing their trio . . .

"Holy, holy, holy,
Lord God Almighty!
Early in the morning our song shall rise to Thee."[1]

For me, God's holiness was connected with the clock ever so slowly ticking out the remaining minutes of the monotonous message while I squirmed on the hard seat searching for relief from the heat and longing to be free from constraint. Do you relate in some way to that picture?

Possibly you think of holiness as a list of rules to freeze freedom and crush your creativity. Maybe you have known some people who claimed to be fired up about holiness, but there's nothing appealing about their lifestyle or perspective on living a God-centered life. They live by black-and-white thinking that says, "This is holy, and that is not." Rule lovers—they delight to point out who is not making the grade on their latest checklist of absolute rules for holiness.

That's not God's kind of holiness.

God does not present His holiness as a horizontal prescription for human activity. God displays holiness as the central and defining essence of His character. I know some people think that God is defined by love, but I would beg to differ. If love was at the very center of God's nature, then He could have welcomed us into heaven without the atoning death of His Son, Jesus. Fact is, God's holiness demanded that sin be paid for, and then His love compelled Him to pay the price Himself.

To know God as He truly is requires dispelling our human notions of holiness and thinking about it in a fresh, new way. Let's start there—with a lofty view of exalted holiness from the God who said, **"Be holy, for I am holy."** When we allow ourselves to be gripped by that reality, no human standard of goodness, no man-made regulation of righteousness, no plastic, legalistic creed will ever again substitute for such a fearful and wonderful encounter.

So let's bag what man says about God's holiness and let the ever-new message of God's Word shape our ideas about Him. The Bible has the power to change our lives by introducing us to a God whom our culture, even our Christian culture, has ignored, softened, and minimized. A true glimpse of God in all His holiness will rock your world to the core. I want that; don't you?

If your answer is yes, then stand with me at the base of God's holy mountain. Warning: There's no way we can scale the heights of holiness in this brief study or even in our short lifetime. After reading the next few pages, we won't say, "Oh, I get it. What's next?" But through the eyes and words of the prophet Isaiah, we can step a little closer. In humble dependence, we can ask God to reveal to us more of His holiness, and I'm confident He will.

GRIPPED BY THE HOLINESS OF GOD

Just to remind you, our man Isaiah flashed like a shooting star over the dark sky of a morally corrupt culture. His specific, God-given call was to minister to the affluent leaders of his day. Isaiah knew what it was like to move among self-sufficient people. They had power, money, and influence—what more did they need? Sound familiar?

I talk to people all the time who have deceived themselves into thinking that they've got life hardwired. They have a good education, a good job, and a good portfolio. Their life is moving along at a pretty good pace, so they think they don't need God.

If I could, I would take these loved ones by the shoulders and shake them . . . hard. I would say, "Do you realize what you are saying?" But since it's not proper for a pastor to do that sort of thing, I'll settle for saying loud and clear, "Wake up, dude! It's not about who *you* are. It's all about who *God* is." That's what Isaiah figured during the event recorded in Isaiah 6:1–7. (Now's a good time to go back and read the passage on the first page of this chapter if you did not do so earlier.)

God allowed Isaiah to peek into His heavenly throne room and glimpse His holiness like no human being has ever done! And he was seriously laid out, or we would say "gripped," by what he saw. Isaiah's vision of this scene above the ceiling is one we desperately, desperately need in the church today. Why? Because it blows away the comfortable, manageable God we've fashioned for ourselves. It reminds us how small we are and how great He is. So great, in fact, that He is unapproachable except in the ways He has prescribed.

Did you ever learn about the children of Israel's desert wanderings? The people and priests understood God's innate holiness far better than we ever have. When God instructed them to build the tabernacle, He included a place for Himself called the Holy of Holies that was so sacred, so ominous that only *one* person *once* a year could enter, and *only* with an offering. The place was filled with such mystery that every year, before that one priest entered, they would tie a rope of bells around his ankle, just in case he did something wrong and was struck dead on the spot. Then the other guys could pull him out of the Holy of Holies without meeting the same end. The priests of old had a mega, reverential awe of God and His holiness.

God is holy, and to see His holiness means to do it His way.

Back then nobody confused the creature with the Creator. God is set apart way above any human standard. Set apart for a special purpose. There was no one like God. That's why this vision Isaiah had of entering God's throne room is so cool. And God invites us, through Isaiah's eyes, into a place very few people have ever been. How many times have we said we want to know God? Well, here's our chance. Let's explore Isaiah's vision one piece at a time.

In the year of King Uzziah's death (v. 1)

The date 740 B.C. may not mean much to you and me, but to Isaiah's original readers, the date marked the end of an era. King Uzziah had been a fixture in Israel, ruling the nation for fifty-two years. For the most part, they had been good, peaceable years. So, when leprosy finally took his life and his long reign ended, the country was thrown into incredible turmoil. Imagine what it would be like if we had a president for fifty-two years and felt secure and accustomed to his ways. Everything is operating like clockwork—then suddenly every television channel interrupts programming with the stunning news from Washington that the president is dead.

When Uzziah died, the nation's moral climate went into a tailspin. People began to think, "If I'm going to make it in this crazy culture, it'll be on my own, doing what I think is right for a change."

In the midst of this moral confusion, God called Isaiah to speak for Him.

In the year of King Uzziah's death I saw the Lord *(emphasis added)*
Think of the significance of those four words. **"I saw the Lord."** Who could ever be the same? Now, whether he was waking or sleeping, whether he had a vision or a dream, we're not told. But Isaiah was supernaturally allowed to see the very throne room of God.

Notice the word "Lord." When it's LORD (all caps), it refers to God's covenant name, Yahweh. But here *Lord* is lowercase, referring not to God's name, but to His position. Isaiah is really saying, "I saw the ultimate Monarch! I saw the Sovereign! The Ruler over everything! I saw Him!"

John 12:41 indicates that Isaiah actually saw the pre-incarnate Christ, the second person of the Trinity. It couldn't have been God the Father, as is commonly thought, since John 1:18 says, **"No one has seen God at any time; the only begotten Son, who is in the bosom of the Father, He has declared Him"** (NKJV). So, Isaiah was allowed to see Christ before His incarnation. Before Jerusalem, before Nazareth, before Bethlehem, Isaiah was given one quick glimpse of Jesus, the second person of the Trinity, in all of His glory . . . and it took his breath away.

. . . sitting on a throne
Notice what Isaiah saw in the next phrase. **"I saw the Lord sitting on a throne."** Sitting—not pacing back and forth. Sitting—not wringing His hands. Sitting—not struggling or searching. Not God. Where was He? He was seated. He was settled. He was secure. He was certain.

I wrote in the margin of my Bible, "Why so settled and so seated?" The answer is: because He is in control. He knows it. Everyone in the throne room knows it. No one is worried.

I am struck by that truth each time we sing a particular worship song at Harvest Bible Chapel. The lyrics include the phrase, "You are in control." When I sing it, I think of this verse in Isaiah. God is seated on the throne. He is in control. Wow, that sure puts into perspective any burden I carry on my heart. How difficult could this problem be for God, no matter how monstrous it might seem to me? What problem would seem large to the One who is *sitting* on a throne? My problems are nothing to Him. He is in control! Even of this? (Think about your biggest worry right now.) Yup. He's even controlling that. Even *this?* (Think about the biggest issue facing our world today.) Even *that.* The Lord is *sitting* on His throne.

. . . lofty and exalted

Notice the Lord isn't just sitting on any old throne. **"I saw the Lord sitting on a throne, lofty and exalted."** I believe that the main reason the church has lost its moral vision is because it has lost its high and exalted view of God. We have embraced the comfort of His nearness at the expense of His transcendence. God is not the "man upstairs." God is not an old codger with a white beard. God is ineffable glory, and He dwells in unapproachable light. The Bible says that no one can see God and live. He is lofty and exalted.

. . . with the train of His robe filling the temple.

The train is the part of the robe that communicates honor. Seldom seen today except at formal weddings, the train is the symbol of grandeur and royalty. If you've ever seen a video clip of the coronation of Queen Elizabeth many years ago at Westminster Abbey, you would remember that the train of her robe went all the way down the aisle and almost to the back door of that cathedral. It took several courtiers to carry the train of her robe during her coronation.

What does Isaiah say about the robe of almighty God? He says it fills the temple! Down the aisle and back again, back to front, front to back, doubling and redoubling. The symbol of God's splendor fills the temple. So awesome is this view of God that Isaiah can look no higher than the train of His robe. Isaiah cannot elevate his eyes beyond the hem of our Lord's garment.

Just imagine, if the *hem* of our God's robe *fills* the temple, think of His presence! Isaiah, so overcome by the sight of this holy God, can only describe the fringe of His clothing. Isaiah is so completely awestruck that he has to look away and says in effect with his next phrase, "Let me tell you about the angels."

Seraphim stood above Him (v. 2)

The seraphim are the angels that exist in the throne room who instantaneously do the bidding of almighty God—ever standing to serve the seated Sovereign. The Hebrew word *seraph* literally means "the burning ones." Though we have more questions than we can answer about the seraphim, we are given a limited physical description of them and their role. Picture two lines of angels coming out from the throne of God, **"each having six wings: with two he covered his face, and with two he covered his feet, and with two he flew"** (v. 2).

Why six wings? Two cover their faces lest they see the glory of God and die. Always serving but never able to look upon the Holy One. Two wings cover their feet which symbolize their lowliness—lest God see them and the shame they feel in the presence of infinite holiness. And with two more wings they flew. It's interesting that four of their six wings are for relating to God; only two are for serving Him.

The verbs *covered* and *flew* are continuous action. The angels' motion is ceaseless as they fulfill with precision every wish of almighty God. And they don't just fly; they speak as they hover around God's throne.

And one called out to another . . . "Holy, Holy, Holy" (v. 3)

You got that picture in your mind's eye of the seraphim forming two lines coming out from God's throne? Now, listen as they call out back and forth, from one line to the other in an antiphonal chorus that through ages of time has gone on without interruption. And what do they say? Imagine all the things they could say about God. They could say, "Merciful, Merciful, Merciful God!" They could say, "Loving, Loving, Loving God!" But God, in a mystery we could guess at but never comprehend, chose that the words spoken continuously before His throne would be of His holiness.

So these burning ones call back and forth, back and forth, back and forth, never ceasing: **"'Holy, Holy, Holy, is the LORD of hosts, the whole earth is full of His glory."**

And this *never* stops. This praise never ceases. It goes on and on and on through countless eons of time. This brings to mind a well-known

Bible teacher who recently visited our church and ridiculed modern worship as a collection of repetitious diddies. How strange that such a good man would not be fond of something God not only appreciates but has ordained, namely the endless, changeless chorusing of a single line of certainty. When the truth is significant, there is great power in repetition, especially if the subject is an attribute of God.

Actually, in the Hebrew language when someone writing or speaking wants to emphasize something, he or she will repeat the word. For example, if they wanted to tell you that they fell into a pit, they would say "pit." But if it was a really deep pit, they would say that they fell into a "pit" pit. While several times in the original language of Scripture we can read a repeated word for emphasis (for example, *shalom,* the Hebrew word for peace used in Isaiah 26:3, is literally "peace, peace," meaning peace now and peace for eternity), nowhere in all of Scripture do we see an attribute repeated *three* times. This three-peat is used only of God and only of this attribute. The seraphim are saying that God is not *just* holy, and not *just* "holy, holy," but that the Lord of hosts is *"holy, holy, holy"!* The whole earth is full of His glory! Think of that chorus as it goes on endlessly and eternally. In fact, it's going on at this very moment. Isaiah stood there stunned and silent as he gazed upon the transforming scene and trembled in the presence of God.

And the foundations of the thresholds trembled at the voice of him who called out (v. 4)

Isaiah, no doubt prostrate by now, was not aware that the whole temple was shaking. It seems he thought just the doorway was shaking as if to say, "This far! No farther! You can go no closer to the holy presence of almighty God."

. . . while the temple was filling with smoke.

Consider the scene. The angels' antiphonal hymn was thunderous. The temple foundation was shaking. Then comes the smoke rising quickly to veil Isaiah's sight. Why smoke? I believe that it was God's protection of Isaiah, lest he be consumed in another moment by the utter terror, by the majestic purity and power, the unsearchable, unspeakable, infinite holiness of the triune God. The smoke graciously shielded Isaiah from a view that no man or woman can see and live (Exodus 33:20).

GET A GRIP ON GOD'S GREATNESS
God's Holiness—Your Model

*I*saiah's favorite name for God is "The Holy One of Israel"—the *Qādash*. By calling Him the *Qādash*, he describes God's character in two seemingly opposite ways:

1. God's holiness evokes awe. He is frightening beyond belief and filled with superhuman and potentially fatal power.
2. God is set apart from all others and evokes our adoration and reverence. It is in this way that we as believers are called to be holy. We are called "saints"—literally the set apart ones.

The apostle Peter tells us to be like God—the Holy One—set apart in everything we do (1 Peter 1:15). He says, Be totally sold out to God! Be available for His special use! Refuse to be entwined in sin. Jesus prayed for you in this same way (John 17:17). He asked His Father to protect you and to sanctify you (set you apart)—so that you would be living pure and ready to be used by God. Imagine that . . . today, Jesus prays that you would be holy.

Now, friend, when was the last time you heard about the incredible reality of God's holy presence? Have you ever fully considered what it means? Preferring the comforting truths of God's love and mercy, we have lost this awesome vision of His holiness. The result is that our faith is too often anemic and malnourished by the spiritual equivalent of junk food. We talk about Him as if He were our buddy. We wallow in sin, and revel in a grace that is cheapened because it is separated from this penetrating, purifying holiness.

We've missed such a huge piece of what it means to be alive and to be men and women connected to God. We have no identity problem when we understand ourselves from God's perspective. Our anxieties and pressures dissipate. When we see God as Isaiah did here, we dip our toes in the greatest experience a human being can have—to stand in the presence of a holy God.

I'll say it again, dear friend: We desperately need to be gripped by this view of the highness and the holiness of God. Because we have failed to let it capture our hearts, we so seldom hear what comes next in verse 5.

ISAIAH'S RESPONSE

Isaiah, watching all of this, finally had to say something. His only appropriate response to the impact of being gripped by God's holiness was **"Woe is me, for I am ruined!"** (v. 5). The word *woe* means literally the calamity has fallen or is about to fall. Malachi 3:2 says, **"Who can endure the day of His coming? And who can stand when He appears?"** Isaiah was saying in effect, "*That's* God? *That's* who He is? I am dust!"

> When we experience God for who He really is, we suddenly see ourselves for who we are.

The same is true today. You cannot gaze upon the holiness of God without being overcome. Even as I've studied this passage over the past several days, I've been deeply impacted. I've thought and studied and reflected on God's holiness, and I've felt wounded by my own sinfulness. How could a person *not* be overcome when confronted with such a holy God? Isaiah was saying in effect, "That's the standard? That's how high the bar is set? If that's true, then I am finished! I am broken! Woe is me!"

David said, **"If You, LORD, should mark iniquities, . . . who could stand?"** (Psalm 130:3). If God were to mark and record every sin that we have committed, who could bear up under that kind of scrutiny? So Isaiah says, **"Woe is me, for I am ruined!"** Isaiah shouted in effect, "I'm dead. I'm done for. I am silenced."

I have to shake my head in grief when I hear people spout, "I don't know what God's doing in this ol' world, but if I ever get a chance, I'm gonna straighten Him out on a few things." And I want to respond, "*What?!* What did you say? Listen up! No one can see God and live!"

If ever for a moment we should get to peek under the corner of the curtain, we would be on our faces before God. Isaiah says, **"Woe is me . . . because I am a man of unclean lips."**

"How can I open my mouth and speak for this God? What could I say about Him?" Isaiah asks. "I am a man of unclean lips. And do you know something else? I dwell amongst a people of unclean lips." We're all so truly sinful before this Holy God—all of us!

God forgive us for thinking, "You know, Lord, I think I'm a bit more holy than some of Your other followers." What a joke! Who cares about how you compare to the other guy? Who can stand before this God? May God forgive us for seeing this chapter title and thinking, "Holiness, oh yeah, maybe there's a couple of things I could dig out and upgrade, but I don't know what they are. I know I'm not perfect, but the fact is I've known the Lord for a long time, and I've come pretty far in—" *In what!?* Who could gaze upon this God and not be overcome with a sense of their incredible, desperate need for a fresh infusion of who He is?

May God help us be a people that will embrace not only the messages about Him that delight our hearts, but also the ones that grip us and shake us to the core of our souls. We'll have to deal with these truths about God for all of eternity; better to start the reality check now, don't you think?

"My eyes have seen the King."

Isaiah said, **"I'm ruined. I'm filthy. I live with unclean people."** Why, Isaiah? Why do you feel so overcome? Because, the prophet writes, "My eyes have seen the King." The king of what? "The *King!*" It's like he said, "My eyes—for a moment before the temple filled with smoke—my eyes saw the *King!*"

Isaiah grieved, "I saw the King, and I knew I was unclean."

What he discovered at a deeper level we all must continually review. We are all immensely unclean before the holiness and righteousness of almighty God. In the purity of God's holiness, our sinfulness is exposed for public inspection.

Then one of the seraphim flew to me. (v. 6)

Praise the Lord for the word *then*. How tragic would it be if I ended this chapter right now and said, "That's the holiness of God—now go deal with it." Instead, one of the seraphim flew to Isaiah "**with a burning coal in his hand, which he had taken from the altar with tongs. He touched** [Isaiah's] **mouth with it and said, 'Behold, this has touched your lips; and your iniquity is taken away and your sin forgiven'**" (vv. 6–7).

There's an incredible lesson here. We are only prepared to receive and comprehend the grace of God when we have understood His infinite holiness and our incredible sinfulness. Any presentation of the gospel which leaves that truth out is incomplete. It's the holiness of God that casts us upon His mercy.

Just in case you missed that last thought, let me repeat it. We are only prepared to receive and comprehend the grace of God when we have understood His infinite holiness and our incredible sinfulness.

Try to remember that the next time you are tempted to gloss over a sin in your life. "Well, it's not that bad." Or "everyone understands." Refuse that trashy kind of rationalization. It belongs in the gutter, for sure. Let's never forget Isaiah's throne-room vision of the holiness of God. Allow God to grip your heart with this truth and you'll find you have no more patience for your own lame excuses!

Make a mental note of this: God calls *us* to holiness. That's why that seraph went to the altar and got a coal to cleanse Isaiah. God wants us to be holy. How incredible is that? *"Be holy, for I am holy,"* God says. "What? Like You? How could that be possible?" Isaiah, overcome with his own sinfulness, begins to experience the grace and mercy that flows from this holy throne.

Let me ask you this: Why did that seraph get the coal? Was it because he felt sorry for Isaiah? Was it because he decided, "Poor Isaiah, he seems to be a little beat. Let's help him"? I would suggest to you that the angel went and got the symbol of cleansing by the direct command of almighty God Himself. I doubt that there is a whole lot of personal autonomy among the angels around God's throne. I'm suggesting they do *exactly* what God wants them to do. Though it's not stated, here we see a God who is infinitely holy yet sees Isaiah, no doubt on his face before Him, and directs the seraph, "Go get a coal off the altar." And the angel goes and gets the coal and brings it to Isaiah for cleansing. That's a picture of our loving, forgiving, merciful God.

On earth, the altar was a place of continual burning, where animals were offered as sacrifice for sin. We can only guess that the altar in heaven parallels that atoning place. Because of His holiness, God will not simply *declare* us righteous in some random act. He will not dismiss our sin without a substitute. It was on that altar where the substitute for sin was made.

He touched my mouth with it.

The angel comes with the coal and *psssssssst*. Purged. Maybe you have felt as you read this chapter that you cannot possibly relate to this holy God. Perhaps there are some things you have done in your life that few, if any, people know about. You feel so ashamed, unclean, and unworthy. But wait—aren't you amazed to discover that in the fullest and most awe-producing vision in all of Scripture regarding God's holiness there is this additional picture of His forgiveness?

Think of it. God Himself sent for the instrument of Isaiah's cleansing and forgiveness. Isaiah was washed clean, cleaner than any launderer can whiten (Mark 9:3). Cleansed, not only of the small and silly but also of the serious and shameful. Wholly cleansed by our holy God.

Now we are at the critical moment. I remember the first time I truly understood that God's holiness was entirely unattainable. That no matter how hard I tried I could never live up to this infinite standard. I learned that because of my sins I was not only ineligible for God's forgiveness but fully deserving His punishment. I was told that two thousand years ago Jesus Christ, God's Son, accepted the punishment for my sin and died in my place. I saw that Jesus gave His life so His holy Father could release me from the just penalty for my sin and grant to me full and complete forgiveness.

Have you come to that understanding? To be truly forgiven, all you must do is turn from your sin and come to Christ by faith. If you have never made that decision, I urge you to do so now. All that God longs to do in your life begins in that moment of conversion (Matthew 18:3). It's a crisis every person must come to, and it doesn't happen by accident. You can't be converted without knowing it any more than you can be married without knowing it. To be converted requires turning from sin and coming to God in faith that Jesus died for you.

What Isaiah experienced from the altar in that moment was symbolic of the sacrifice of Jesus once for all (1 Peter 3:18). And it can be yours in this moment if you embrace by faith the forgiveness God freely offers in Christ (Romans 6:23).

CONVERTED FOR HOLINESS

Contrary to popular opinion, God does not offer to forgive us simply so we can come to a crisis of conversion and receive the eternal benefits of His forgiveness. God cleanses us because He wants to transform us, to make us holy just as He is.

For a moment, let's fly over to a New Testament passage that completes this truth. First Peter 1:14–19 says,

> *As obedient children . . . like the Holy One who called you, be holy yourselves also in all your behavior; because it is written, "You shall be holy, for I am holy" . . . knowing that you were not redeemed with perishable things like silver or gold from your futile way of life inherited from your forefathers, but with the precious blood, as of a lamb unblemished and spotless, the blood of Christ.*

So this infinitely holy, immeasurable, unalterable, unfathomable God says, "I've cleansed you for holiness." Think of that. "I want you to be like Me—holy. I've done what you could not do so you would have this incredible opportunity to be holy—now go for it."

Wow! "Be holy, for I am holy." That's a high call. I cannot attain unto it. I feel like this silly little boy standing at the base of Mount Everest considering a climb. "Be holy, for I am holy." You've got to be kidding; how could I ever . . .?

It Happened to Me

SABBATICAL REVIVAL

Yes, a personal encounter with the holiness of God did happen to me and has many times over. The real turning point, however, came on a beach on the south coast of France.

The year was 1998, and I was thirty-eight years old. Ten years had been logged as a senior pastor. Our elder board, sensing my complete exhaustion, had graciously allowed us a three-month sabbatical. I got as far away from the pressures of ministry as I could.

In that place of rest and restoration, I could finally bring God the questions that were plaguing my mind. Why are people who claim to love You so harsh and unforgiving? Is it right that people so aggressively and ungratefully harvest the benefits of a person's strengths and then so vocally lament their weaknesses too? *"Man, why don't they get a mirror and take a look at their own lives?"*

Of course, this hurt was coming from just a few people; by far the majority of people I was working and worshiping with were wonderful in every way. But those few . . . made me sick of the "heat." And that summer, I wanted "out of the kitchen." If I did go back, it would be to something very different.

Inside, I was weary and wondering how I could go on with such fear in my heart. Yes, I was scared, so much so that I hadn't even told my wife the depth of my disillusionment. But I had sure told the Lord. I came to Him with all my despair. I was looking for comfort, but instead I found conviction . . . about the sin of people pleasing. I was searching for hope, and God showed me His holiness. First slowly, and then with strength and supernatural force, God gripped my heart with His holiness.

Early one morning I was walking on the beach, listening to Scripture, and pouring out my heart to God. God's Spirit began to speak to my spirit in a way that wouldn't be any clearer if it were audible. His questions began to displace my own perplexities. "Why are you so focused on others? Am I not the One you have chosen to serve?" Jesus' words to Peter in John 21 came with force, **"What is that to you? You follow Me!"** *(v. 22). And the Lord said to me, "Yes, others are hypocritical, but are you not the same?*

Do you practice all that you preach? Are you so far above others that you cannot give grace as I give it to you? I am the standard! Holiness is My nature, and you're not coming close!"

In a matter of moments I was on my face in the sand behind some rocks and spilling my tears into the ocean. "I saw the Lord, high and lifted up." Not the God of the quick answer and the catchy praise chorus. Infinite, unapproachable holiness. As the waves close by crashed on the shore in the background of my hearing, wave after wave of God's holiness crashed upon my heart. What right do I have to question His calling? I have no choices—only to trust and obey a God who miraculously even takes notice of one like me.

God's holiness became my goal and consuming purpose—not managing human opinion, not keeping a record of wrongs, not juggling private sin and personal rationalizations. All these lessons this preacher should know and did, but I needed to be gripped. I needed God's Spirit to take me and shake me about real holiness. The God-kind, pure and penetrating, powerful and infinite.

With the waves of realization came a deep heart commitment to give up "trying" to live the Christian life. That moment became a turning point for my whole understanding of how the holy character of God is formed in a believer. (See page 32 in my book I Really Want to Change . . . So, Help Me God.)

I came to see that holiness is character before it is ever conduct. It is the very nature of God reproduced in the heart of man. It is the engine that fuels all lasting happiness.

Christianity in not a prescription for behavior; it is a holy encounter.

Though I've since had my moments where human opinion has encroached, I can say from my heart that I was changed that day. I am stronger and more secure in my true purpose for existence. I am forever changed by the sea of holiness I saw on the south coast of France. It happened to me.

I began this chapter sharing the distorted perception I had of God's holiness as a child. I didn't understand that the process of holiness is the pathway to happiness. I had to learn that God's holiness is not some abstract character trait to be admired like a fine painting or an antique car. What God forbids as sin He does because He knows us. Every time God says "Don't," what He really means is "Don't hurt yourself." When we choose to sin, we choose to suffer. All the pain and suffering in our world is the result of humanity rejecting this call to holiness. But you can accept it today. You can embrace the reality of God's transforming work unto genuine, lasting, joy-producing holiness. God knows this kind of joy infinitely and eternally.

RESPONDING TO GOD'S HOLINESS

Are you gripped by the awesome reality of this truth about God? Will you let the holiness of our awesome God take you and shake you so that you can never see temptation as tempting again? We said we wanted this study of God's holiness to change us, so let's start here and now. Begin by rejecting the kind of surface adjustments that substitute for holiness in so many corners of Christ's kingdom. That may be God's wake-up call to you. Or perhaps you need to examine if a hyper-grace mentality has eclipsed your vision of an exalted and holy God, who is calling you to live a lifestyle that is truly set apart for Him! As you are forgiven and cleansed, I challenge you to be finished with rationalizations and hypocrisy. They have no place before a holy God! As we invite God to grip our lives with His holiness, let's respond to Him with a passionate pursuit of genuine Christlikeness. Like Isaiah, let's purpose to shine like a meteor against the night sky of the moral darkness in our world. And together let's pursue lives and lifestyles that proclaim with integrity the infinite holiness of our great God.

LET'S PRAY

Holy God,
    Please forgive me for my casual attitude about sin. Action sin. Thought sin. Speech sin. Forgive me, God, for hiding my behavior behind Your abundant grace. Help me to embrace from my heart a season of transformation. No more duplicity and hypocrisy. No more playing church and playing Christian. I want the real thing, Lord.
    Oh God, I want to see You reigning, not just upon Your throne, but in my heart, in my life, in my home, and in my relationships. Pursue me with a desire to be like You that I cannot outrun. Be

specific with me, God. I invite You to be high and lifted up, reigning upon the throne of my heart. This I pray in Your name.

—*Amen.*

MAKE IT PERSONAL

- This Sunday as you attend a worship service, imagine the scene Isaiah described—the Lord seated on His throne and in full control. Whatever burden you carried into the service, lay at His feet and direct your focus toward His majestic holiness.

- What's been your take on holiness? Do you tend to be a rule-lover, or does your pendulum swing more toward freedom and not enough behavioral boundaries? Consider what it means to be holy, "set apart" for God in practical ways. Ask God to help you choose your convictions, attitudes, and actions based on His defining holiness.

- Examine your daily habits with a willingness to change anything that doesn't reflect God's holiness in your life. What do you need to lock out of your life—some viewing habits on the web, television, or video? Is it the way you spend your money or maybe the way you respond to those who hurt you? What do you need to limit— what is stealing your hunger for God? What habits do you need to eliminate completely? Holiness calls for radical change.

- Refuse shallow, one-way thinking about God. Live with the tension that God's holiness creates a distance between Him and His people. We are dust in comparison to His glory. His ways are unsearchable, incomprehensible, incomparable, great, wonderful, and exalted. Worship Him for who He is in all His holiness.

The Awesomeness of God

Behold, the Lord GOD will come with might,
With His arm ruling for Him.
Behold, His reward is with Him
And His recompense before Him.
Like a shepherd He will tend His flock,
In His arm He will gather the lambs
And carry them in His bosom;
He will gently lead the nursing ewes.
Who has measured the waters in the hollow of His hand,
And marked off the heavens by the span,
And calculated the dust of the earth by the measure,
And weighed the mountains in a balance
And the hills in a pair of scales?
Who has directed the Spirit of the LORD,
Or as His counselor has informed Him?
With whom did He consult and who gave Him understanding?
And who taught Him in the path of justice and taught Him knowledge
And informed Him of the way of understanding?
Behold, the nations are like a drop from a bucket,
And are regarded as a speck of dust on the scales;
Behold, He lifts up the islands like fine dust.
Even Lebanon is not enough to burn,
Nor its beasts enough for a burnt offering.
All the nations are as nothing before Him,
They are regarded by Him as less than nothing and meaningless.
To whom then will you liken God?
Or what likeness will you compare with Him?
As for the idol, a craftsman casts it,
A goldsmith plates it with gold,
And a silversmith fashions chains of silver.
He who is too impoverished for such an offering
Selects a tree that does not rot;
He seeks out for himself a skillful craftsman
To prepare an idol that will not totter.
Do you not know? Have you not heard?
Has it not been declared to you from the beginning?
Have you not understood from the foundations of the earth?
It is He who sits above the circle of the earth,
And its inhabitants are like grasshoppers,

Who stretches out the heavens like a curtain
And spreads them out like a tent to dwell in.
He it is who reduces rulers to nothing,
Who makes the judges of the earth meaningless.
Scarcely have they been planted,
Scarcely have they been sown,
Scarcely has their stock taken root in the earth,
But He merely blows on them, and they wither,
And the storm carries them away like stubble.
"To whom then will you liken Me
That I would be his equal?" says the Holy One.
Lift up your eyes on high
And see who has created these stars,
The One who leads forth their host by number,
He calls them all by name;
Because of the greatness of His might and the strength of His power,
Not one of them is missing.

The most eloquent mouth could never

express . . . the most intelligent mind

cannot comprehend . . . how incredibly

awesome God is!

Chapter Two

GRIPPED
by the
AWESOMENESS
of GOD

Isaiah 40:10–26

GOD IS AWESOME!

Most of us get the idea, we just don't have a clue about the magnitude of His awesomeness.

When we call something awesome these days, we mean "cool" or "wow" or "what an upgrade!" *Awesome* is our label for everything superlative.

The lid on the cookie jar slams, and I hear "Mom, these cookies are awesome."

Your coworker praises you, "Awesome job on that project!"

A neighbor kid brags, "Check out my boom box—the subwoofers are awesome!"

Then we come to church and sing, "Our God is an awesome God," and wonder why our worship falls flat.

We've ruined another word.

God is awesome indeed, but our flippant use of the term has made it as interesting as vanilla. At best, a cliché.

Only when we encounter the One who is truly awesome—only then are we speechless. We have no words left that belong to Him and Him alone.

But maybe speechless is the best way to approach God's awesomeness. By far, I think this unique aspect of God's character is His coolest. Everything that is God is awesome, and everything that is awesome *is* God. At my house, you're not allowed to use "awesome" for anyone or anything *except* God. It's the rule . . . because it's the truth. To call anything else awesome is a joke. The real kind of awesome sends shivers up your spine.

> God's awesomeness takes you to your knees in total reverence, to worship without self-consciousness and to walk in glad surrender.

At the risk of sounding simplistic, *awesome* means "producing awe." Look it up; you won't find any warm, soft synonyms for awe. They're serious and threatening. Awe promotes fear and terror. Dread and fright. Awesome says, "Watch out!"

Hebrews 10:31 says it right: **"It is a terrifying thing to fall into the hands of the living God."**

But the flip side is that when you are gripped by God's greatness, His awesomeness runs like a river of joy through the very center of your being. You know beyond any doubt that you were created for Him, for this moment.

Isaiah knew all about God's awesomeness. He proclaimed it without apology to an apathetic and aggressively wicked audience. Within the limitations of language the Holy Spirit gave Isaiah the greatest description of God's awesomeness ever penned; his words are God's words about Himself, and they are worthy of our careful study.

CLEAR THE WAY FOR GOD TO WORK

I've got to warn you. We each have obstacles in our lives that hinder us from hearing God's Word. That's why Isaiah begins chapter 40 with **"Clear the way for the LORD in the wilderness; make smooth in the desert a highway for our God"** (v. 3). When it comes to communicating with His people, God wants nothing to hinder His truth from reaching you. He wants every single obstacle out of the way. So what's blocking His access to your life? Could it be *you?* Are you trying to work things out on your own, refusing to let God's awesomeness shake you out of your self-defined comfort zone? Get out of His way! Perhaps other people are hindering His truth from reaching you. Or perhaps you've talked about your problems till you're weary of your own voice—still, no answers.

I challenge you to stand still in the severity of the moment and let God's awesome power transform your perspective.

In these beginning verses of chapter 40, Isaiah tells of another voice that says, "Call out." And we would then ask, "'What shall I call out?'" How could we possibly find words to describe an awesome God to our generation?

Isaiah felt the same way as he said, **"The grass withers, the flower fades, when the breath of the LORD blows upon it; surely the people are grass. The grass withers, the flower fades, but the word of our God stands forever"** (vv. 7–8).

He's right. Our words are like grass—they dry up and blow away. But God's Word endures forever. Let's dive into what God says about Himself in the Bible.

WHICH GOD DO YOU KNOW?

Isaiah begins his description of God with what sounds like a contradiction. Most people know either the God of verse 10 *or* the God of verse 11. Which side of God's nature are you most familiar with? But both are true. Both are powerful.

In his first description, Isaiah writes:

Behold, the Lord God will come with might, with His arm ruling for Him. Behold, His reward is with Him and His recompense [justice] before Him. (v. 10)

Do you know the God who rolls up His sleeve, bears His powerful arm, slams it on the table, and says, "C'mon people—get it together! Live right." Have you experienced that strong arm of God?

Good! But if that's all you know, then be gripped by His other arm described in verse 11:

Like a shepherd He will tend His flock, in His arm He will gather the lambs and carry them in His bosom; He will gently lead the nursing ewes.

In other words, God is a shepherd, scooping up His lambs and carrying them close to Him. God provides special treatment for special needs. At certain times your shepherd would say, "This one is hurting. Careful of his wound. We're going to have to carry her for a while." This tender arm of God reminds us of His unique and personal care for us.

God has two arms . . .

One arm is mighty and powerful, demanding holiness and righteousness.

One arm tenderly cares for the weak and wounded.

Almighty and tender . . . one awesome God. We'll talk more about that later.

THE WHOLE EARTH IS YOUR CREATION . . . GOD, YOU ARE AWESOME!

This may sound silly, but take a good look at your hand. Hold it out. Inspect your fingers and your palms. Pretty useful tools, aren't they? Maybe that's why Isaiah uses them to describe creation. He tells us that God is one **"who has measured the waters in the hollow of His hand, and marked off the heavens by the span"** (v. 12).

"Measured the waters." Cup your hand. Look at that little place down there in the middle. Think about all of the water in all the world—God measured the oceans from the hollow of His hand. To be a little more exact, that's 912,500 cubic miles of water. That's a mile by a mile by a mile, 912,500 times. And God's like, "Got it right here in My palm."

"And marked off the heavens by the span." The span of your hand is the distance from the tip of your thumb to the tip of your baby finger. In biblical days, a hand's span was a common measuring tool.

I can almost get my span around an orange. You try it. You've seen Shaquille O'Neal on the basketball court, right? He could probably get his span around half a basketball. God, on the other hand, can palm the world. God says, "See the Earth? It's 25,326 miles all the way around—got it right here in My palm!"

And it's only because of His mercy and patience that He doesn't slam dunk us all. Doesn't that blow you away?

Next Isaiah tells us that God "calculated the dust of the earth by the measure." Ever try to move the dirt around in your backyard? Amazing to learn that in creation our awesome God laid down all the soil on the whole planet and said, "That'll be about a cup, thank you." And it's done.

Notice also the agency of God in creation; He is calculating, measuring, spanning. Those who would say that somehow God began some evolutionary process and then withdrew haven't understood Isaiah 40. Clearly, God spoke the world into existence. He was personally the agency and the instrumentality of its creation.

With all my heart, I believe that God did all this in six literal twenty-four-hour days. I'm not troubled by scientific skeptics who think they know more than what God's Word says. The historians, geologists, and evolutionary scientists of the world have often challenged the Bible, only to be proven wrong. It's almost laughable to think of them trying to figure out God's program. I'm going to stick with what God has said in the matters yet to be verified by science. I'm sure He's not holding His breath, waiting to be validated. As if, "Whew, they've finally proven I'm real; what a breakthrough!" I don't think so.

Notice God's majesty in the next phrase. **"And [He] weighed the mountains in a balance and the hills in a pair of scales."** Picture the mountainscapes of the world. God said, "OK. Put the Rockies on this side of the scale. Bring them up into Canada. Now let's make the Himalayas. How big do We want those? There . . . there, balance them out, and, yes, done!"

Now, friend, isn't *that* awesome? Doesn't that make you feel tiny?

Let's jump down to verse 21. I love Isaiah's attitude here.

Do you not know? Have you not heard? Has it not been declared to you from the beginning? Have you not understood from the

foundations of the earth? It is He who sits above the circle of the
earth, and its inhabitants are like grasshoppers, who stretches
out the heavens like a curtain and spreads them out like a tent
to dwell in. (vv. 21–22)

You can almost hear him say, "Duh! Haven't you heard? Where
have you been?" If you feel small when you imagine God's creation,
it's because you are! God says we're like grasshoppers! Picture yourself on a hot summer night out on the deck with your family and
friends having a barbecue. How much do the grasshoppers in your
lawn affect your evening? A little background noise maybe? Hardly a
distraction. That's the entire human race before God and His awesome
purposes.

Now look at verse 22. **"It is He who sits above the circle of the**
earth." Twenty-two hundred years before Christopher Columbus, God
said our planet was circular and not flat. Here it was in God's Word all
along. Ditto on the science versus Scripture comment above. I'll go
with God's explanation every time.

THE HEAVENS ARE YOUR HANDIWORK . . . GOD, YOU ARE AWESOME!

But God **"stretches out the heavens like a curtain and spreads**
them out like a tent to dwell in" (v. 22). The word *heavens* describes
all of God's created universe. He said, "Now, let's make the universe,"
and *poof* . . . as easily as you put up an umbrella, it was all there.

Do you have any idea the immensity of the universe God spoke into
existence? I've tried for many years to find a decent description. Try this
on for size: We're on planet Earth, and we are 93,000,000 miles from
the sun. Imagine that distance as the *thickness* of a piece of paper. From
the Earth to the sun, 93,000,000 miles equals a piece of paper.

With that in mind, the distance to the nearest star is a stack of
paper seventy-one feet high, with every single piece of paper representing 93,000,000 miles. (Stay with me; this is getting outrageous.)
The size of our galaxy is represented by a stack of paper 310 *miles* high
(the distance from Chicago to St. Louis), with every single piece of

paper in that stack representing 93,000,000 miles. That's just our galaxy, and it's one among millions.

You say, "Oh, I understand that." Well, think about this then.

The *known* universe is a stack of paper 31,000,000 miles high with every single piece of paper representing 93,000,000 miles! Now for those of you who like math, there are 10.4 million sheets of paper in a stack one mile high. Therefore, the known universe is 31,000,000 miles of paper, with each mile representing 10.4 million sheets of paper and each sheet of paper representing 93,000,000 miles. Are you getting a headache?

In every description we see of God's reality, we are struck by the immense distance that exists between us and God—in power, in size, in ability, in majesty. The gap is too great to measure. This must be what the astronauts felt viewing the Earth from the moon's surface. We are so small . . . so infinitesimally tiny. God, on the other hand, could inhale the universe in a single breath. The writer of Hebrews understood this. Check out Hebrews 1:10–11:

> *You, Lord, in the beginning laid the foundation of the earth, and the heavens are the works of Your hands; they will perish, but You remain; and they all will become like a garment, and like a mantle You will roll them up; like a garment they will also be changed. But You are the same, and Your years will not come to an end.*

In other words, God can roll up and toss away the universe as easy as rolling up an old shirt. The immensity of it all is really so much more than we can grasp. That's why we reserve the word _____ (fill it in yourself) just for Him.

THE NATIONS ARE YOUR INSTRUMENTS . . . GOD, YOU ARE AWESOME!

A drop in the bucket—you've heard that expression. It means *almost nothing,* like $100 to the national economy. *Bloop,* "just a drop in the bucket." That's what God thinks about the nations who disregard His awesomeness. Of course there are a lot people who don't give a rip about God's Word or His invitation of grace. Did you ever wonder what God thinks about them? Verse 15 makes it pretty clear that the feeling is mutual. Isaiah says, "Behold, the nations are like a drop from a bucket." They are like a speck of dust on the scales, Isaiah goes on to say.

All the nations are as nothing before Him, they are regarded by Him as less than nothing and meaningless. To whom then will you liken God? Or what likeness will you compare with Him? (vv. 17–18)

Isaiah is beginning to stutter as he tries to think of words to shatter man's tiny perception of God. He's not like this . . . and He's so much bigger than that . . . and so far beyond—??? Then what can we compare Him to? How can we describe how awesome He truly is?

And to that question, we . . . we have no words.

RULERS ARE MERELY PUPPETS . . . GOD, YOU ARE AWESOME!

Worried about world powers? World War III? Terrorists? Market crashes? Biological warfare? Understand this: "[God] **reduces rulers to nothing**" (v. 23), and He regards them as **"less than nothing and meaningless"** (v. 17).

Not one of His purposes is ever delayed or frustrated— not even for a moment.

Whatever happened to Napoleon? Didn't he die in exile on an island somewhere? Or Alexander, the not-so-Great? Hitler? They're dead. Or the maniac leaders of our generation, such as Osama bin Laden? Oh, they're still around? Maybe for ten more minutes! Their influence is hardly a blip on God's monitor. They may cause us to bite our nails and worry, but God isn't pacing or wringing His hands. Just as soon as He's ready, He will reduce those leaders to nothing, and He will do it with His feet up.

Isaiah says in effect, Don't you get it? God doesn't read the *New York Times*. And if He did, it wouldn't make any difference. *Nothing* stops God's unalterable purposes in this world!

I can't wait for that day in heaven when we get to hear history's real story—when we read God's script and realize all He was doing behind the scenes. Just imagine the drama of God's continuous, all-wise intervention in the sinful machinations of human armies and governments. We will be amazed, stunned, and captured by God's awesome control of human affairs.

Verse 24 says of world rulers, **"Scarcely have they been planted, scarcely have they been sown, scarcely has their stock taken root in the earth."** God just expels a breath and . . . **"But He merely blows on them, and they wither, and the storm carries them away like stubble."** When will we embrace the reality of God's awesome control over history? History is and always has been God's ball game. He decides who pitches, who scores, and who gets on base. He calls one man out and advances another runner. Awesome!

IDOLS ARE A CHEAP SUBSTITUTE BECAUSE . . . GOD, YOU ARE AWESOME.

I think this is the funniest part of the whole chapter. Man thinks, *I can't control God. I can't understand God. I'm just going to make my own god.* So Isaiah deals with the idol thing once and for all.

> *As for the idol, a craftsman casts it, a goldsmith plates it with gold, and a silversmith fashions chains of silver.* (v. 19)

Can you imagine some guy calling his wife from work, "Hey, Martha. I'm going to be home a little late tonight; I have to make god." But he's not making just *any* god—Isaiah says a goldsmith puts gold over it, and a silversmith adds *silver.*

Isaiah's sarcasm makes me laugh. **"He who is too impoverished for such an offering selects a tree that does not rot"** (v. 20). The tongue-in-cheek description is obvious. "If you can't afford a gilded god, then send today for a god made out of heavenly mahogany carved by the kingdom's most skillful craftsmen. Don't delay! This holy knick-knack is guaranteed not to wobble or fall down. Get yours today for $39.95." Do you see how ludicrous that is?

Don't miss the application for each of us. Idols are not just in

Isaiah's day; nor are they only in the African jungle. We've polished our image a bit, but idols still serve as cheap substitutes for God. Things like my career, my bank account, my children, my marriage, my investments, what I'm going to do with my life, not to mention every false religion on the face of the planet.

In our foolishness, we build our lives around our self-made gods. I say it's time we let God be God as He has revealed Himself in His Word! That means embracing everything God says about Himself rather than making Him what we want Him to be—that is, crafting our own little idol. We can't make Scripture an a la carte menu. "I'll take a generous portion of the comforting, fatherly God as my main God, with a little lovey-dovey, man-upstairs God on the side, but hold the judging, holy God. Last time I had Him, I had trouble sleeping!"

Why would we settle for some sugary dinner-mint religion when we can have an eight-course meal of the only God who is?

LOOKING FOR SOME WISDOM? . . . GOD, YOU ARE AWESOME!

If there was one thing I could ask for and receive each time I faced a problem, it would be God's wisdom. Like you, I long to know the wisest response, the best direction, the perfect choice in many circumstances I face. As I seek the Lord in prayer, I am reminded that He's got it all figured out. Always has. Always will. And wait—we can ask Him for wisdom! (James 1:5).

Look at verse 13. **"Who has directed the Spirit of the LORD, or as His counselor has informed Him?"**

That's a rhetorical question if there ever was one. God has never been informed or taught about anything. God has never said, "You're kidding Me!" *Never!* No one has ever given God an angle on any subject or took Him aside for a verbal upgrade. Not once!

Let's play a game. I'll ask the rhetorical questions from verse 14, and you give the answer.

With whom did He consult?	*(No one.)*
Who gave Him understanding?	*(No one.)*

Who taught Him in the path of justice
   and taught Him knowledge?   *(No one.)*
Who informed Him of the way of understanding?   *(No one.)*

No one influences God. No one impacts the Lord. No one changes His mind about anything. He doesn't need you, me, or anyone.

When we hear that, our natural response is "Don't I matter at all to God?"

That's not the point.

The point is that God loves you and me because He chooses to.

Get rid of the twisted thinking that God loves you because He saw something in you that attracted Him. That may be the way human relationships work. "God cares for me because I am a hard worker or a caring neighbor or a faithful parent." Wrong! He loves you because He chooses to.

At first that's hard to take. "I want God to care for me because He really likes me." But if God only loves us because of who *we* are, then we have to lie to ourselves about who we are in order to receive that care. He doesn't love you any more or any less because of who you are or what you do. He loves you to the max simply because in His mercy He chose to.

Do you see how freeing that is? Any risk you have of losing God's love goes out the window. You can never be outside His circle of love, because it's not about you—it's about Him.

BIGGER THAN I IMAGINE
AND NEARER THAN I THINK

That takes us to one last and very important truth about God's awesomeness, and again, it has two parts—both critical to understand.

On one side is God's transcendence. It's what we've been covering throughout this chapter. God is wholly beyond us and completely above us. He is completely *not* like us. He is bigger and more powerful and more awesome than we can ever imagine. No one can see God and live, **"for our God is a consuming fire"** (Hebrews 12:29).

Now, if God's awesomeness was only seen in His transcendence, then we would have no relationship with Him. How can you know and fellowship with the powerful and completely independent God of the universe? Fact is, we could not apart from His equally awesome *imminence*. Imminence is like the little sticker on the passenger side mirror of your car that says, "Objects in this mirror are closer than they appear." The Bible teaches that in spite of God's mighty transcendence, He is very near to each one of us, even this very moment.

I am thankful for the comfort of God's nearness, but it breaks my heart to hear His imminence preached in so many churches to the exclusion of His awesome transcendence. Then all we end up with is a teeny-weeny little God who might be imminent (i.e., close), but totally impotent. So let's get these two truths into alignment with each other and our own hearts. Like two towers that can never be toppled, God is both imminent *and* transcendent. Ominous . . . and near. Out of this world . . . yet as close as your next breath.

GET A GRIP ON GOD'S GREATNESS
God's Awesomeness—Your Shelter

In the Bible, God's awesomeness and His name *Almighty* often go together. Almighty is translated *El-Shaddai* in Hebrew, which literally means "God of the Mountains." Every time you read about God Almighty, think of His mountainlike majesty, in whose presence there is a "secret place" or a shadow. In His awesomeness, you can also find shelter. When the psalmist needed protection in times of need—he went to God, his awesome mountain of safety. You too have this place of refuge in God's awesomeness. Memorize Psalm 91:1 so you know where to run when you need a shelter: **"He who dwells in the shelter of the Most High will abide in the shadow of the Almighty."**

EVEN IN TRIALS, GOD IS AWESOME!

In view of God's compassionate, attentive imminence, Isaiah insists that the people stop saying, **"My way is hidden from the LORD, and the justice due me escapes the notice of my God"** (v. 27). He's like, "Time out! Everybody knock off the whining and saying dumb stuff that isn't even true." I know you may feel like God has forgotten you. I realize circumstances may even lead you to doubt Him—*but God has not forgotten you,* and you must believe that.

It's good to remember at this point that Isaiah was writing to a people who have just been told they were going to suffer incredible persecution as a discipline from God. What was their crime? Simple —they forgot who He was. They lost all sense of proportion regarding God's greatness. *God's presence demanded awe, and they yawned.* For multiple generations they had rebelliously, willfully, happily done their own thing—and God was like, "Enough!"

Now Isaiah's audience cried out for the Lord. They asked, "Where is He when we need Him?" Isaiah's saying, "He's right where you left Him. He's not moved an inch."

Like Isaiah's original audience, we live in decadent days among a people who have disdained and diluted the biblical concepts of God. Let Isaiah's message of God's awesome nature blow across your parched heart and bring refreshment to your soul.

"Tell them," God said through Isaiah, "hard times are coming, but don't give up—now or ever. Don't let them underestimate My power to reorder the universe. Tell them to keep trusting Me and living the way I told them to in spite of what's coming."

How can they? How can you or I? By getting a grip on God's awesomeness.

I love what Isaiah says next. **"Do you not know? Have you not heard?"** (Didn't you get the memo?) **"The Everlasting God, the LORD, the Creator of the ends of the earth does not become weary or tired"** (v. 28). Remember, He's not like us. He never gets tired. He never feels overwhelmed.

"His understanding is inscrutable" (v. 28). You know . . . I'm not going to even touch this one. How could I unscrew the inscrutable?

And besides, how great would God be if average intellects like yours and mine ever got a total handle on who He is?

He gives strength to the weary, and to him who lacks might He increases power. (v. 29)

When your battery is running low, God knows it! Some people might say, "I don't really need God's strength. I have my own program." You are so wrong!

As a pastor, I often interact with people who boast, "I have my act together. I have a career plan and my education, and I'm heading in a good direction. My future's bright." Listen, please. Surrender your pride before God brings you low. You will never break God's back, but He will break yours. You will not deny His purposes. If you don't bow your knee before Him willingly, He will force you to your knees. Believe me, you want to get low on your own.

So let's all admit it together—**"though youths grow weary and tired, and vigorous young men stumble badly"** (v. 30), everyone needs God. Even the strongest. Even the youngest. The sooner you learn that, the less pain you will experience.

You say, "Well, how do I get that strength?" Last verse. Here's the promise: **"Yet those who wait for the LORD will gain new strength; they will mount up with wings like eagles, they will run and not get tired."** You recognize that verse, don't you? Did you realize that its context surrounds the awesomeness of God? You may say, "Wait? I don't have time to wait. I drive fast, eat in a hurry, talk without taking a breath—I'm living in the fast lane. Don't make me wait." Sorry! God says *wait*.

"But are God's ways worth the wait?" I can't believe you're asking that after we've spent the entire chapter detailing His awesomeness. The answer, of course, is yes. He is worth it. We easily forget how great God is. Perhaps we should take time intentionally just to remember that.

A PERSONAL CHALLENGE

I invite you back to a time when your soul was gripped by the awesomeness of God. Where were you the last time you stood in breathless wonder of God's creation? Were you standing on the rim of the Grand Canyon? Or dangling your feet off a mountain precipice? Were you stargazing at a million lights? I remember a time I was drifting in a quiet canoe with nothing on the wind but an orchestra of birds; I could hear the rustle of trees and see their reflection on the shimmering water. I was on a wilderness trip in northern Ontario, Canada. Miles from anything fake or manufactured, the stuff God made was magnified in all His awesome splendor.

It's time to do it again—probably way past time. Make a date with your Creator. Get alone with the God Almighty of the universe. Revel in His awesomeness. Remember His mighty acts. Call back to your mind the great things He has done in your life. All of creation is designed to point you to Him. So, wait silently before Him and allow yourself to be shaken by His greatness, lost in the wonder of His majesty and awesome power.

Isaiah directed you to do just that. Look at verse 26:

> **Lift up your eyes on high and see who has created these stars, the One who leads forth their host by number, He calls them all by name; because of the greatness of His might and the strength of His power, not one of them is missing.**

Remember God's awesomeness every evening when you see the night sky. He knows each star by name. Because of the greatness of His might and the strength of His power, not one of them is missing. Awesome!

And remember . . . His love and care for you is a million times greater than that.

It Happened to Me

LANDON

On February 3, 1988, our second son, Landon, was born. We had done our best to prepare for him. Our little seminary apartment had bulged its second bedroom to squeeze a crib in beside big brother's bed. I was working as full-time pastor/full-time student, and Kathy was a full-time mother/ ministry wife and part-time nurse during the evenings I was home.

Though he was rather "blue" as he entered this world, the hospital staff quickly got him breathing and crying, and his parents wept for joy at the sight of their second son. After all the excitement, I went home to get some sleep.

Imagine my shock to return to the hospital by early afternoon and find my wife dressed and packed, sitting on the bed with a Kleenex in hand to wipe away the quiet stream of tears. What??? I needed the words repeated so I could soak them in.

"They have taken Landon by ambulance to Lutheran General's neonatal intensive care unit (NICU). He was turning blue and couldn't breathe; they were going to find the problem and do what they could."

Do what they could? Every pastor who visits the hospital knows what those words mean and the answer is hardly ever good. As the minutes turned to hours, the diagnosis was firm and grim. Diaphramatic hernia! It's a condition quite rare where the diaphragm doesn't close and keep the intestines below the stomach. Floating upward during gestation, the intestines force the heart to the right of the chest and compress the lungs in such a way that they cannot properly form. On Landon's X-rays we could see that his left lung was almost non-existent, and his right lung was far below capacity.

As we entered the newborn intensive care, he was lying in one of those plastic trays under a heat lamp—a picture deeply etched in the memory of every parent who has traced those steps. We heard the report that 88 percent of children born with this condition do not survive the first twenty-four hours and struggled to accept the nurses' near-verdict that he "might not live through the night." Moments later, we sat in our car outside the hospital with empty arms and heads bowed in trembling prayer to an awesome God.

"Lord, we do not understand why this is happening. We bring our fears and heartache to You. Somehow You have allowed Landon to be born to a circumstance where only You can help him. We want to accomplish something for our new son that is so far beyond us we can only turn in faith to You. We are asking for You to heal him. Use the doctors, use the medication, use what You will, but cause his organs to be realigned and his lungs to be reformed, and he will belong to You, for Your purposes and for Your plans. If this is not Your will, Lord, help us to accept what You have planned . . ."

As I closed my prayer and released my clasp of Kathy's hands, we both experienced what we had only heard reported: God's incredible peace that truly "passes understanding."

A sleepless night brought the relief of some morning duties at the church. I was buoyed to know that the good people of Arlington Heights Evangelical Free Church, along with countless family and friends, were holding us up and asking God for a miracle in the life of a baby boy they had never seen or met. As Landon struggled through the night, striving for every breath, the surgeons prepared for the surgery. Before the sun was up, his little chest was opened wide and his intestine tucked back below his stomach. The diaphragm was sewn shut to hold it all in place, and they closed his chest with heart and lungs still so misplaced, knowing his little life could handle no more.

We arrived at the hospital to all this news and the critical need for more prayer that Landon's limited lungs would give enough air to sustain life for a second surgery and protect him from brain damage. The next three days were agonizing. But alongside the stress was an outpouring of prayer like we had never known before. Christians from around the continent were kneeling in prayer to an awesome God, asking for a miracle. Every nurse and doctor must have known of our faith as they witnessed the steady stream of phone calls and visitors and saw us time and again in the glow of that heat lamp huddled and holding hands around our son, calling out to our awesome God.

By the fifth day, Landon was strong enough to face the second surgery, and because the parents in such a setting are given great latitude, I was actually standing beside Dr. Jae in the NICU prior to the surgery as he saw the X-ray for the first time. He looked puzzled and confused, straining to comprehend what he was seeing. He tore the X-ray off the lighting device to examine more closely the corner of the film containing the patient's name. Confirming that it was in fact the X-ray of our son, he puzzled a moment more and then turned to the intern struggling with me to comprehend the doctor's actions. "And what's wrong with this patient?" he barked in an almost angry tone.

The intern looked at the X-ray, moved in close for a better view, and after an agonizing silence reluctantly admitted, "I don't know."

"Right!" the doctor said, "Nothing!" And with that he slammed his fist on the X-ray machine, cutting the light, and briskly exited the NICU.

The X-ray revealed that his displaced heart, which they had hoped to delicately move through a second surgery, was in its rightful place. A miracle, beyond description and irrefutable. Landon's left lung, which the doctor had earlier described as more of a "node" due to a lack of space to form and grow, was rightly placed and full of the squiggly X-ray lines that reveal a nourishing flow of air. Another miracle.

The few babies who survive this birth defect spend weeks or months in the NICU, but Landon was home in his crib by the end of the seventh day. An irrefutable miracle from an awesome God. An answer to prayer undeserved but mercifully given so that God's awesome character could be reported to you today.

Months later, a friend of ours heard our doctor speak at a medical colloquium. When asked about the unexplainable in the field of medicine, Dr. Jae reluctantly told the story of Landon's healing in detail, admitting that sometimes "medicine meets marvels that defy explanation." A human description of an awesome God. As I write this, we're planning Landon's seventeenth birthday celebration tomorrow. How do I know that God is awesome? . . . It happened to me!

TIME TO GIVE IT UP!

Maybe you find as I do that when your heart is gripped afresh by God's awesomeness, there's nothing left to do but resign your life to Him. You hear His call to "lay it all down" and experience the joy of total, unqualified surrender.

If you make that decision, if you follow through and really begin to live the life that is totally and completely submitted to God's awesome purposes, I want to make you a promise.

When my kids were small I used to tease them relentlessly. They ate it up, and I sure had fun. The problem came when I wanted to teach them something. They couldn't grasp the transition from silly to serious. To rectify that problem, I made a commitment to them: When I used the words "I promise," it meant I wasn't kidding. In our home those words mean, "Relax; I guarantee I'm telling the truth." Just the two words "I promise," and the kids could be 100 percent sure that Dad wasn't teasing anymore.

I'll say it again. If you fully and sincerely submit to God's awesome purposes in your life, you will never regret it—no, not for a moment. . . . I promise!

LET'S PRAY

Awesome God,

Through this study, You have become very large in my eyes. Your awesomeness has been magnified before me. Your transcendence is so much more than I imagined, and Your nearness is so much closer than I thought. You are awesome, God. Your comfort and strength are all that I need.

Please give me the faith and courage to take my eyes off these challenges I face today. At times, they are all that I see. They've become so big as to eclipse any view I have of You and Your power. I surrender these burdens to you now—especially these . . . (God loves it when we are specific in prayer).

Thank You for inviting me to draw near to You. It amazes me that in Your infinite power, You still want my fellowship. Increase my faith so that I grasp Your greatness as a current experience. Bring Your glory to bear upon my life so that others see Your name lifted up as never before! I praise You and adore You. I worship You, almighty God.

—Amen.

MAKE IT PERSONAL

- Are you facing a difficult decision or season of your life? Get a grip on God's transcendence and imminence. With His one arm, He is able to break through any barrier, overpower any obstacle; yet with His other arm, He is tenderly caring for you as a loving shepherd. Could anything be too hard for Him? Instead of succumbing to our natural tendency toward self-pity or defeat, allow yourself to be embraced by the arms of God. Stand confident in this trial, knowing that God sees you, God can do anything, and in some mysterious way, He is working all things together for His glory and your good. Spend some time today writing out the awesome things that you have personally seen God do in your lifetime. State why you believe the author was God. Then reaffirm your faith in God's awesomeness because of all He has done and will do for you.

- Make a date with the Creator. Go somewhere to view a wonder in His creation. Take your Bible with you. Sit in silence, guarding your mind against mental distractions. Sit there at least a half hour (or more). Don't try to tell God anything; just be available to Him. At the end of your time, quietly (or maybe loudly!) sing some of your favorite songs of worship. Sing to Him! Read Psalm 8 in closing. (Maybe begin to memorize its nine verses to give to Him in worship on your next time alone with God.)

- When the evening news troubles you with its reports of world rulers out of control and murderous senseless conflict between nations, return to Isaiah 40 and remember that nothing can be done outside of God's almighty plan. No event in human history is outside His influence even in the slightest. No world ruler can change God's program. Do not fear! God Almighty is working out His awesome plan.

- Here's an exercise you can try alone or with your family/friends. God's awesomeness embraces so many of God's other attributes. Invent a memory device to summarize a part of God's character. For example, awesomeness is **A**ltogether **B**eyond my **C**omprehension (A B Cs). Or use the letters in your family's name to remind you of God's greatness. (Kids will love this.) Try giving the acronym and then letting the kids guess what it stands for.

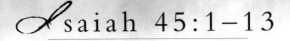

Thus says the LORD to Cyrus His anointed,
Whom I have taken by the right hand,
To subdue nations before him
And to loose the loins of kings;
To open doors before him so that gates will not be shut:
"I will go before you and make the rough places smooth;
I will shatter the doors of bronze and cut through their iron bars.
I will give you the treasures of darkness
And hidden wealth of secret places,
So that you may know that it is I,
The LORD, the God of Israel, who calls you by your name.
For the sake of Jacob My servant,
And Israel My chosen one, I have also called you by your name;
I have given you a title of honor though you have not known Me.
I am the LORD, and there is no other;
Besides Me there is no God.
I will gird you, though you have not known Me;
That men may know from the rising to the setting of the sun
That there is no one besides Me.
I am the LORD, and there is no other,
The One forming light and creating darkness,
Causing well-being and creating calamity;
I am the LORD who does all these.
Drip down, O heavens, from above,
And let the clouds pour down righteousness;
Let the earth open up and salvation bear fruit,
And righteousness spring up with it.
I, the LORD, have created it.
Woe to the one who quarrels with his Maker—
An earthenware vessel among the vessels of earth!
Will the clay say to the potter, 'What are you doing?'
Or the thing you are making say, 'He has no hands'?
Woe to him who says to a father, 'What are you begetting?'
Or to a woman, 'To what are you giving birth?'"
Thus says the LORD, the Holy One of Israel, and his Maker:
"Ask Me about the things to come concerning My sons,
And you shall commit to Me the work of My hands.
It is I who made the earth, and created man upon it.
I stretched out the heavens with My hands

And I ordained all their host.
I have aroused him in righteousness
And I will make all his ways smooth;
He will build My city and will let My exiles go free,
Without any payment or reward," says the LORD *of hosts.*

God's sovereignty is first painful, then

slowly powerful, and only over much time

seen to be profitable. It is to be studied

with great sensitivity for the experiences

of others and deep reverence for the One

who controls the outcomes of every

matter in the universe.

Chapter Three

GRIPPED
by the
SOVEREIGNTY
of GOD

Isaiah 45:1–13

GOD'S SOVEREIGNTY has gotten a bad rap lately.

Let's say tragedy strikes—something big like what happened on December 26, 2004, in Southeast Asia when a powerful tsunami wave swept more than 200,000 men, women, and children to their deaths. Maybe someone you love dies very suddenly, or test results indicate you're the one scheduled for the early exit. Then, before the impact of the tragedy has gone from your head to your heart, some goody-two-shoes, wannabe theologian wraps his overly familiar arm around your shoulders and whispers words intended to comfort, but instead they cut like a knife. "God is sovereign; all that He allows is for a higher good."

The implication is that you should swallow hard, because in the end you'll realize that the torpedo that just blew a hole in the side of your boat was for your benefit.

I hate that! What's the devastated person supposed to think? If that's all I knew about God's sovereignty, then I would conclude, "God is good sometimes, but He's cruel other times. I guess you just can't trust Him."

That is not true, but it will take me a few pages to explain. Stick with me here.

Let's start with a foundational truth—God's display of His sovereignty *is* scary sometimes, but only because it's so not like us. Sovereignty is all about being God. We reduce Him

In our need for control, we want a God who is manageable.

to some heavenly pal or celestial bellboy. We want to use the Lord like a rabbit's foot. Someone "lucky" to hold on to when the dam breaks and the water's rising. In some twisted way, we think we're more secure when we've got God figured out.

Sovereignty says, "No way!" There's no way you're going to figure out God. He's more than we might dare to imagine.

Here's another hard fact: When it comes to how He directs the people and events of history, God doesn't need our permission. Hate to tell you, but He's not going to stoop down and explain why He's doing everything He chooses to do. With both the macro- and the microscopic world under His constant control, God is able to do *whatever* He pleases *whenever* He wishes. I want you to remember this when we get to the end of the chapter, because there's something very comforting I want to share then. For now, let's agree—God is way beyond our figuring out. That's not only OK . . . that's the way it needs to be.

Can you imagine how small God would be if we could comprehend all that He allows and why? What if the smartest and wisest of all mankind ran the universe; can you imagine the cosmic mess we would be in? It only makes sense that an element of mystery surrounds God's person and His ways.

In the next few pages, we're going to circle the base of the mountain of God's greatness, this time with His sovereignty in mind. Clouds block our view of the complete picture, and even up higher when we break through the clouds, we discover we're only in the foothills. God is so much greater than us. Beside Him, we stand so infinitesimally small . . . Let that sink into your soul, and you'll begin to feel a surprising comfort.

GOD'S SOVEREIGNTY EXPOUNDED

The term *sovereignty* means "independent." That means:

- God is the Ruler of all.
- God answers to no one.
- God can accomplish whatever He wants—in all things.
- God sees history from beginning to the end. No obstacle or adversary can hinder His plan from happening.
- God is afraid of nothing. Ignorant of nothing. Needing nothing.
- God always knows what's best, and He never makes a mistake.

Sovereignty means God is in control of it all. He's over things we see and things we don't see. Stuff we understand and stuff that if we even glimpsed it for a second would blow us away. Sovereignty means it's all His. Nothing can stop what He purposes from happening. Not people, events, or time. Get it? What God plans, He delivers. What God wants, God gets—His way and His timing, on time, every time. That applies to what you're going through today and what was happening to Isaiah back in chapter 45.

Thus says the LORD to Cyrus His anointed (v. 1)
At the time Isaiah wrote this section of his book, the Babylonian Empire covered all the countries in the news today: Israel, Iran, Iraq, Saudi Arabia, Syria, Turkey, etc. Nebuchadnezzar, the king of Babylon, invaded Jerusalem, conquered the people, and devastated the temple, taking all of the items of worship. In addition, he took captive the choice young men from the nation of Israel and made them court slaves (eunuchs, gulp!) back in Babylon.

After Nebuchadnezzar came other kings: Darius, Belshazzar, and his father, Nabonidus. You can get a firsthand account of this whole period by reading the book of Daniel; the prophet experienced the whole thing.

Toward the end of Daniel's life came the Medo-Persian Empire. On October 12, 539 B.C., an army led by a Persian king named Cyrus marched on Babylon and swallowed the whole empire. Before the month of October was over, Cyrus faced his captives and said in effect, "I'm the new king on the block, and things are going to be different around here. I am going to be your savior and deliverer."

Cyrus released all the deported Israelites, allowing them to flee Babylon. In one day, fifty thousand Jews returned to their homeland. This is significant! If that release had not happened, it's very doubtful a nation of Israel would have existed in Christ's day, let alone in ours. All that God wanted to do in bringing the Messiah into the world hinged on this pagan king, Cyrus. Cyrus didn't love or submit to God in any way, but God used him. That's why God called Cyrus "His anointed."

> God can use anyone and anything to accomplish His ultimate purposes.

That word *anointed* is the same word that is translated other places in the Bible as *Messiah*. The idea is that God is so completely sovereign and entirely in control that when He wants to get something done, He can even use a person who hates Him to accomplish His sovereign will. Remember what we said? Nothing can ever stop or slow God's sovereign purposes.

So 150 years before the events happened, God revealed to Isaiah the details surrounding Israel's return to the land. We study Isaiah 45 as history; Isaiah spoke it as prophecy. He even gave the exact name of the ruler that God would use. I'm guessing when Cyrus showed up in Babylon, Daniel smiled with the scroll of Isaiah in his hand.

Here is how God described Cyrus: **"Cyrus [My] anointed, whom I have taken by the right hand, to subdue nations"** (v. 1). Cyrus might have thought he was the one conquering empires, but God says, "You're just a little boy. I was leading you by the hand."

God told Cyrus he was appointed to **"loose the loins of kings; to open doors before him so that gates will not be shut"** (v. 1). God also said, **"I will go before you and make the rough places smooth; I will shatter the doors of bronze and cut through their iron bars. And I will give you the treasures of darkness and hidden wealth of secret places, in order that you may know that it is I, the LORD, the God of Israel, who calls you by your name"** (vv. 2–3).

Interestingly, we have no indication Cyrus ever came to any kind of a faith relationship with the one true God. But still, God sovereignly used him.

Why did God do it? "For the sake of Jacob My servant, and Israel My chosen one," God says. From the first chapter of Ezra we learn that Cyrus was so generous to the Jews he actually stormed the treasury in Babylon and gave back their golden instruments of worship which Nebuchadnezzar had taken more than a century earlier. "Not only can *you* go back," God is saying, "but I'm returning all of the treasures stolen from you." How they must have rejoiced on the journey home to have seen God's sovereignty so up close.

Back home to Israel they went to live as a free people once again. All because of God's work through pagan king Cyrus. That's why He says in verses 4–6,

"I have also called you by your name; I have given you a title of honor though you have not known Me. I am the LORD, and there is no other; besides Me there is no God. I will gird you, though you have not known Me; that men may know from the rising to the setting of the sun that there is no one besides Me. I am the LORD, and there is no other."

That Scripture passage rocks, doesn't it?

To sum up: God is the ruler of the universe, and He is the king of human history. *Nothing* happens in this world by chance. Nothing! Forget about luck. There is no such thing as coincidence. Only this sovereign God who rules over all that we are and do. I love that last line of verse 6—**"that men may know from the rising to the setting of the sun that there is no one besides Me."** Wow!

While Napoleon was leading his armies over much of Europe, they won *astounding* victories. At one point, someone was heard to say to Napoleon, "Is God on the side of France?" In other words, how could all of these victories be taking place but that God must be doing this?" In his arrogance Napoleon said, "God is on the side that has the heaviest artillery." But then came the Battle of Waterloo where Napoleon lost both the war and his world. In very short order the entire empire collapsed on his head.

Years later, while he was in exile on the island of St. Helena, he was reported to have quoted the words of Thomas á Kempis, "Man proposes, but God disposes." We can fire up all kinds of dreams and ideas, even spend ourselves trying to see them happen, but the "end game," as they say, is all about a sovereign God. Our only real choice is whether we are for Him or against Him. And amazingly He can work His purposes regardless of the choice we make.

GET A GRIP ON GOD'S GREATNESS
Your Master—the Sovereign Lord

*L*ord GOD. We throw God's title around like we're on a first-name basis. Yet Isaiah calls God the reverential name *Adonai Yahweh. Adonai* speaks of God's unlimited authority; *Yahweh* reminds us of His covenant relationship—the intimacy He has with His people. Out of absolute reverence for God's sovereignty, Jews will not pronounce *Yahweh,* God's personal name, but substitute *Adonai* in its place.

They recognize that the God who dwells in unapproachable light (1 Timothy 6:16) is not to be messed with. He is larger than life. He is bigger than the universe. But He is also Yahweh, the God of mercy who revealed love to His people.

The call to every believer is to live with that tension—not only is He the friend who sticks closer than a brother (Proverbs 18:24) but He is sovereign Master of the universe. **"Thus says the LORD, your Redeemer, and the one who formed you from the womb, 'I, the LORD, am the maker of all things, stretching out the heavens by Myself and spreading out the earth all alone'"** (Isaiah 44:24).

THE SOVEREIGNTY OF GOD EXPLAINED (A BIT!)

How could we ever explain the sovereignty of God? Of course we cannot, but we can share the light Scripture gives us in Isaiah 45:6–7:

"I am the LORD, and there is no other, the One forming light and creating darkness, causing well-being and creating calamity; I am the LORD who does all these."

Underline that second part; He is "**causing well-being and creating calamity; I am the LORD who does all these things.**" When I was preparing this study of Isaiah, I asked our pastoral staff to help me identify the key passages our people would most benefit from. We read the book of Isaiah together, and most of our pastors strongly agreed that Isaiah 45:7 was a verse that was both perplexing and powerful. They wanted me to teach it because they felt that many people struggle with the relationship between an all-powerful God who claims to be loving yet doesn't stop suffering. In reality God does far more than fail to stop human hardship; the Bible says He *causes* it. Yes—read it again: "**I am the LORD, and there is no other, the One forming light and creating darkness, causing well-being and creating calamity; I am the LORD who does all these.**"

It's an amazing statement. We love the good news. Everybody is in favor of the God who says, "I am the One who causes well-being." But most of us struggle with the God of the Bible who goes on to say, "Wait! I'm not *only* the author of well-being; I'm the One who creates calamity." Whoa. How can we marry those two?

Here's the truth: God created a world in which we have the freedom to choose right or wrong, good or bad, sin or righteousness. God is not the author of sin, but He is the One who created a world in which we can choose. And from our choices flow the sin and suffering we see all around us. Much of the pain in our world is the direct consequence of individual sin, such as murder, greed, and hatred. But there is also the suffering we all must bear as members of a fallen race. The effects of a sinful humanity show up randomly in human sickness, natural disasters, and the very process of aging itself. While God does not hurl these hardships at individual people or nations, He most often refuses to prevent the fallout from a fallen world. In that sense it can accurately be said that God is the author of a world in which calamity does strike.

In spite of that reality, the world He made is a good one for all who receive the gifts He offers freely. Into this world of sin and suffering

God does not hesitate to say, "I'm the One who made the world this way, and if you trust Me you will see that My plan is good."

He brings *eventual* well-being for those who turn to Him, regardless of any hardship He may allow, but *eventual* calamity for those who reject Him, regardless of how well their immediate life may be going.

> God ensures His desired ends regardless of the choices we make. His total and complete sovereignty blows the circuits of our finite minds.

As I write this, I'm praying for a married couple on our church staff. Last weekend they received news that the wife's father had suddenly died of a heart attack. They're not completely sure whether he knew the Lord, though they had shared and prayed with him many times. In the midst of this heartache, the wife was at the very end of her pregnancy. Two days after her dad's death she went into labor and delivered a healthy baby girl. Imagine the conflict of emotions: grief weighing heavy on her heart at the death of her dad and joy as she brought her daughter into the world.

We're quick to embrace the God who calls Himself the author of life. "Yes, that's God! God's the One who brought that beautiful baby into the world." But wait. God is also the One who took that father out and said, "His days are completed." Then we begin to say, "God, how could You allow that to happen? Why now, God? Why at the same time?" And we poke our bony finger in the face of a sovereign God. What audacity!

You may wonder, "Is it wrong then to ask questions?" No, asking questions is essential to a growing faith, provided you look for and discover the wonderful answers that are available and then let the mysteries that remain be just that—mysteries hidden in the heart of sovereignty.

TWO QUESTIONS ABOUT GOD'S SOVEREIGNTY

The fact that God sometimes shows us His purposes but then often does not raises two questions. One is theological—a thinking question; the other is very practical—a question of the heart that addresses how we feel. Let me try to answer them both.

First, the theological question: If God really controls all things, then how can He hold us responsible for the sinful choices that we make? In other words, if God is really sovereign and in control, then do I have a free will? Do I choose to sin, or does God determine that I will sin? Am I strung up like Pinocchio, under the hands of some mega-Geppetto? Let's try to answer that, and then we can look at the heart question that naturally follows.

1. Am I just a puppet?

Joshua stood above the nation of Israel, lifted his voice, and called upon them saying, "Choose this day whom you will serve. Choose!" (See Joshua 24:15.)

Moses called out to the entire nation of Israel, "See, I have set before you life and death, blessing and cursing. Choose this day. Choose!" (See Deuteronomy 30:15–20.)

Jesus stood on a grassy hill in Galilee and said, **"Come to Me, all who are weary and heavy-laden, and I will give you rest"** (Matthew 11:28). Our same Lord also called out to the massive crowds that heard Him preach, "Whosoever will may come." Now, is that nonsense? Was Jesus saying, "Whosoever will may come," but under His breath snickering, "that is, if I called you. Otherwise you are so up the creek"? No—that's ridiculous! Obviously, Christ was teaching that we have a choice to make.

You absolutely have a choice . . . Christ calls and we choose if we are going to respond.

"But wait," I hear you say. "Ephesians 1:11 says that God determines all things according to the counsel of His will." That's true too. And you're like, "James, you're giving me a headache." Right. Both of these things are true. *Both of them.* Neither one of them can be diminished. God is absolutely sovereign in all things. We also have a free will to make life choices for which we will give an account.

You say, "Can you explain that any more?" Not really. Remember, the top of the mountain is in the clouds—I can only explain what God has chosen to reveal, right? Deuteronomy 29:29 says that **"the secret things belong to the Lord our God, but the things that are revealed belong to us and to our children forever"** (ESV). There are a small number of truths in the Bible that are difficult to reconcile within the

What About Calvin?

As I am writing about our choosing, I can hear some of you saying, "But what about Calvin? And, don't you believe in T-U-L-I-P (which includes, under *I*, "irresistible grace")? 'Cause if you don't, you don't really believe in sovereignty." Listen, I am sure John Calvin was an OK guy. I think it would be great to have coffee with him in heaven and talk about all the stuff he got from Augustine, etc. But Calvin is not in the Bible. I am not loyal to him, and neither should you be. I am not of Apollos, and I am not of Paul (1 Corinthians 1:12), and I am not of Calvin or Scofield or Charles Hodge. (But I hope to hang out with them too.)

I am of Jesus Christ, and I am of the Word of God. The faith *once* for all delivered to the saints (Jude 1:3). Don't allow anyone to intimidate you into thinking they have a higher view of God because they focus on certain portions of Scripture at the expense of others. Above all, don't get caught up subscribing to a theological system that seeks to put scaffolding around the Bible and God in a box.

There are things God has not explained, and there are tensions between some of the truths He has revealed. Those tensions are called mysteries. To live with them comfortably, just try to remember that He is God and we are not.

limitations of our own minds. These are the secret things that belong only to God. There is far more benefit in focusing on the things which *have* been revealed by the Lord.

What I can do is share two illustrations that have helped me relax about it. By the way, I'm not embarrassed to tell you that there is some stuff about God that I don't get. I'm more concerned when I hear people talk like they have it all figured out. It really bugged me when I sat in seminary classrooms and heard arrogant people say, "I've got it; the tension is resolved; it goes like this . . . !" Throughout church history, people who have tried to solve the tension between the sovereignty of God and the free will of man have ended up with a pile of Scriptures they constantly repeat and a second pile they seem to ignore. Man's free will and God's sovereignty are two parallel lines that meet only in the mind of our Creator, a paradox we *will never* fully comprehend in this life. So listen—*both* are true.

Here's the first illustration. Imagine we are taking a cruise to England. The ocean liner has left New York harbor enroute to Liverpool. Nobody is going to stop it. Yet here we are on the boat. You and I are playing a little Ping-Pong, and other people are swimming in the pool. Passengers are doing their own thing all over the boat. Each is operating as a free moral agent making choices. Yet the choices we make don't affect the fact that this ocean liner is going to England, and nothing is going to stop it. In that way, God has set some sovereign purposes in this world. The little choices that we make will never alter His purposes. I choose what to do on the boat, but either way it's going to England.

> God completely controls the universe—with His feet up! He's not stretched or stressed in any way. That's what it means to be sovereign.

Here's the second illustration. A few years ago I was in Indonesia and got to play against a chess master. I'm a lousy chess player, and it was brutal. There were ten of us, each with a chessboard set up, and he played us all at the same time. He would walk down the row of boards, crushing each of us with his speed and incredibly insightful moves. In fifteen minutes, we were all out of the game. It was crazy!

In some ways that's a bit how God works. We make our moves, but God's purposes are not affected by them. If we make a good move, God knows the next move. If we make a bad move, God knows instantly what He will do. In fact, He has always known both what we would choose and what He would do. But don't think that God is playing a game with us. God made all His moves in eternity past! We're stuck in time; God is not. He's not limited to our little life calendar. He is eternal.

But that may not be where you struggle with the issue of God's sovereignty. It may not bother you to think that God controls consequences and that God produces outcomes. What may disturb you is not God controlling the results of your actions.

Can I guess where it is you might struggle with sovereignty? Is it when painful circumstances come that are not the direct result of choices you have made? That issue gets us to our second question about sovereignty.

2. How can a loving God allow so much human suffering?

God's love is not a pampering love. God's love is a perfecting love. God does not get up every day trying to figure how He can plant a bigger smile on your face. God is in the process of growing us and changing us. His love is a transforming love.

Hebrews 12:6 tells us that **"whom the Lord loves He disciplines, and He scourges every son whom He receives."** In fact, if you are without God's discipline, the Bible says that you are not really one of His children. So sometimes within the framework of sovereignty, God's love says, "I will allow this for a particular purpose." Preferring the meaningful worship of a few to the robotic worship of the masses, God chose to make a world in which people would have the freedom to follow or reject Him. In making that world God knew that some would reject Him, and all of the pain in our fallen world would be the result.

Sometimes God takes hold of that "fallenness" and uses it to chasten and grow His own children. He offers His comforting, abiding presence to His children who endure the exact same kinds of things as those who know nothing of His mercy and grace. God gets glory through the hopefully superior ways His children endure the suffering of this sinful world. So bad things *do* happen to good people. God is sovereign even over that.

Helen Rosevere was a British medical missionary to the Congo during the uprising of the Mau Mau revolutionaries. Though she had gone to the Congo to serve God and to share the gospel, she was personally and brutally attacked. This pure, gracious, innocent woman of God was humiliated and raped, but hung on with her life to a faith in God that refused to be shaken.

While she was recovering from this horrible event, Helen leaned hard on the Lord. That's always the way, isn't it? As you go through a painful circumstance, you either get closer to the Lord or further away.

Trials will always push you. Either they wedge between you and God, pushing you from Him, or the weight of those same burdens drives you closer to Him. If today you are broken, feeling crushed by the weight of a trial, you have a choice. You can harden your heart and refuse the sovereign purposes of God that will one day prove good, or you can run to Him and participate in the blessing God has planned. Can I help you make that choice? Choose to bury your face, even your tears in the mystery of His sovereignty. It's a hard choice, but one you will never regret.

Recovering from her ordeal in the Congo, Helen wrote a statement that each of us should consider. She wrote a question as though spoken from God's own mouth: *Can you thank Me for trusting you with this experience even if I never tell you why?*

Can you thank God for trusting you with the hardest part of your life?

Sometimes we act as the mighty inquisitors, demanding to know why: "*Why* did You do this?" We foolishly say, "I *won't* trust You if You don't show me why!" We expect that somehow God reveals the answers and conforms His behavior to our narrow intellects. What we fail to see is that we are the ones who are on trial and that our incessant questioning reveals more about us than it does about God.

The great Scottish author George MacDonald said, "I find that doing the will of God leaves me no time for disputing about His plans." For some right now that's tough to hear, it may even feel punishing, but God is giving you grace and time to sort these things through. With His help you can get to sovereignty even if the top of that mountain is swallowed up in the mist of mystery.

GOD'S SOVEREIGNTY IS EVERYWHERE

Where does this issue most clearly show up in our world? The best place is on the evening news. We watch the transfer of power from one nation to another and the displacement of once "invincible" rulers—all of this is God's sovereignty at work. What about the war on terror? What about Israel's leadership? To those who think they are independent of a sovereign God, Isaiah answers, **"He it is who reduces rulers to nothing, who makes the judges of the earth mean-**

ingless. . . . Scarcely has their stock taken root in the earth, but He merely blows on them, and they wither, and the storm carries them away like stubble" (40:23–24).

Yes, God is sovereign in world events—yesterday and today!

God is sovereign in salvation.

Isaiah says, **"Israel has been saved by the LORD with an everlasting salvation"** (45:17). God is the One who saves. As one of the billions of people on this earth, if your eyes have been opened to the truth that can be found only in the gospel of Jesus Christ, if you've turned from your sin and embraced Christ as the only basis for your forgiveness, let me tell you, you are numbered among the few on the narrow road to eternal life. The fact that you are off the broad road to destruction is a sovereign act of almighty God.

You say, "But I chose. I chose!" Yes, you did. But somehow in all of that, God was choosing too. Jesus said no one comes unless the Spirit draws him (see John 6:44). In His grace, God sovereignly chose to set His love upon you (Deuteronomy 7:8). If you are among the few who truly know Him, consider yourself among the most blessed of people in history.

God is sovereign in sanctification.

This is the rub. *Sanctification* is the term that describes the process by which God takes converted sinners and transforms their character. If you're in Christ, that's the program you're on. God is sanctifying you; He is changing you. Look at Isaiah 45:8–9:

"Drip down, O heavens, from above, and let the clouds pour down righteousness; let the earth open up and salvation bear fruit, and righteousness spring up with it. I, the LORD, have created it. Woe to the one who quarrels with his Maker."

Underline that last line. It's a pronouncement of judgment. What do you think it means to *quarrel with God?* Isaiah draws two pictures to answer that question.

*"An earthenware vessel among the vessels of earth! Will the
clay say to the potter, 'What are you doing?' Or the thing you
are making say, 'He has no hands'? Woe to him who says to a father, 'What are you begetting?' Or to a woman, 'To what are you
giving birth?'"* (vv. 9–10)

We would never look at a newborn baby and shriek to his or her
parents, "Who made this hideous child?"

Nor would a vessel on the potter's wheel come to life and say, "Get
your hands off me; I don't want a handle *there!*" Isaiah wanted to il-
lustrate how ridiculous we sound when we try to direct God's hand.

Remember Bill Cosby's famous line for parents and kids in conflict? "Watch out, child—I brought you into this world, and I can take
you out." We laugh, but that's parental sovereignty! God is sovereign. He breathed life into us, and He sustains it every moment. If you
draw another breath in this moment it's because He approves. All
that we are always has and always will belong to
the sovereign King of the universe. That's why we
must try to avoid flippantly asking, "What are You
doing?"

Look at the verse again. "Woe to the one who
quarrels with His Maker." After fifteen years of
pastoral experience, I can report this as the place
where most people struggle spiritually. God has allowed some hardship into your life. Maybe it's
your work situation. Maybe it's a marital struggle,

Are you going
to embrace the
life your
sovereign God
has allowed?

or a prolonged health crisis. You could be facing a profound loneliness that won't go away or a deep and sudden loss that time will never completely fill. The choice is easy to understand but terrifically
difficult to make and stick with. It's this: "Either I'm going to get bent
and eventually bitter, or I am going to allow God to be God."

I know these questions are not easy, but they beg the asking. Are
you going to embrace your life situation as something that God has
sovereignly allowed? Will you trust that He will bring a good purpose through your yieldedness to Him? Or are you going to fight and
resist and spend your whole life wondering why you can't be the lady
across the street?

When most people think of Corrie ten Boom, they think of a courageous older lady in sensible shoes and a beehive hairdo who traveled the world in the 1950s to 1980s sharing with millions God's message of forgiveness. But don't think that Corrie's message of forgiveness came easily to her. Corrie's battle to accept God's sovereignty had been fought in the living hell that was the Ravensbruck concentration camp during a war that took the life of everyone she loved. Before Corrie's sister Betsie died, she had described God's sovereignty in a way that changed Corrie forever. "I don't know why God allows suffering, Corrie; all I know is across the blueprint of our lives, God wrote the word *Ravensbruck*. . . . Tell them, Corrie—tell them that no pit is so deep that God's love is not deeper still. They will listen to you because we have been here."

None of us get to choose the words that are written across the blueprint of our lives. The only choice we have is whether we are going to submit to a sovereign God or shake our fist and demand answers not intended for this life. That's the choice we get. Corrie later said, "The higher the view we have of His sovereignty—that our times are in His hands—the greater will be the possibility to live in His victory." The choice that you make at this point determines the person you are for the rest of your life.

Remember, the same sun that melts the ice also hardens the clay. The difference between people is *not* the circumstances that we go through, but how we choose to deal with those circumstances. That's what determines who lives on the peak and who lives in the valley. The good news is that you can make your choice this moment.

GOD'S SOVEREIGNTY EMBRACED

It all comes back to this truth about the sovereignty of God. So let's do this—let's explore three ways we can choose to embrace God's sovereignty.

If you're serious about submitting to His hand, commit these three principles to heart:

1. *I will be obedient when told.* In your heart determine that "when God's Word says something, I will obey it. When God's Word

says 'go here,' I'm going. When God's Word says 'wait or trust,' that's what I'll do. When God's Word says 'live in this righteous way,' I'm going after that with my whole heart."

2. *I will be righteous when tempted.* "God, I want to be a righteous man/woman." We all have temptation points when we feel pulled toward sin. You know what you struggle with, as do I know where I'm weakest. The next time you're tempted, remember Isaiah 45:8: **"Drip down, O heavens, from above, and let the clouds pour down righteousness; let the earth open up and salvation bear fruit, and righteousness spring up with it. I, the LORD, have created it."** God uses the earth metaphorically to picture the righteousness that springs up in our lives when we have victory over temptation. It's a virtual garden of righteousness!

God says in Isaiah 66:2, **"To this one to whom I will look, . . . who is humble and contrite of spirit, and who trembles at My word."** God is promising that He totally takes care of those who embrace His plan and His Word. Remember, willing obedience reveals a heart that is embracing sovereignty. And God says in Isaiah 45:8 that it's His responsibility to fill your life with righteousness. The choosing is yours, but the righteousness itself comes from Him. Consecrate yourself afresh to be the person, the man or woman who God has created you to be. Commit to choosing righteousness when you are tempted.

3. *I will be submissive when tried.* This is perhaps the most difficult of the three principles. In the midst of the trial say, "I'm going to submit to God even though I don't know why He has allowed this and I don't know what He is doing. I am going to humble myself before God and believe He has a purpose I will someday understand. I reject bitterness and hard-heartedness, and I choose to become submissive and wait."

Yet when you willingly take from God's hand whatever He allows, believing that eternity will prove His wisdom and goodness even though you can't see it now, you are embracing sovereignty at the deepest level. And you are preparing your life for a joy so immense that few ever truly experience it. I know this to be true because . . .

It Happened to Me

DENNIS

My wife, Kathy, came to know Christ at fifteen years of age. She was raised by divorced parents, neither of whom had a faith during her childhood. By high school she was living with a father who was living for his only daughter and pouring all of his immense love and affection into the only human relationship that mattered to him. A laborer in the construction field, he left their home early but was always there to greet her warmly and introduce an evening of meaningful conversation and discovery. On weekends they were shopping or at the beach or visiting a museum. Each hour together was filled with wise, worldly counsel about life and men and priorities and how to be a successful woman in a man-centered world. Those who knew them well witnessed a father-daughter relationship most families only dream of.

At some point in the spring of Kathy's fifteenth year, her father decided that she "needed some religion in her life." Though she owned a Bible, she had never read it and could not remember entering a church in her entire life— not even once.

When a believing aunt was to be singing in a local evangelical church, Kathy's father took her to church, seeking to round out Kathy's cultural experience by exposing her to a classical concerto. In God's sovereignty, this was the church I attended, and I was struck with Kathy the first night I met her. Invitations to our youth group came through her cousin, and Kathy's father allowed the limited exposure, considering it a harmless effect that could be easily overcome by his own influence if she ever became truly interested in "religion."

I was in the audience a few weeks later as Kathy's heart was penetrated by the power of the gospel, and she stood to publicly acknowledge Christ as her personal Savior and Lord. In quick time Kathy's loyal father began his efforts to dislodge in his daughter what he viewed as an emotional extravagance. The Spirit of Christ now resident in Kathy's life would not yield to his persistent persecution, and their relationship struggled under the weight of Kathy's new first priority.

About a year later we started dating, and during the next five years of ups and downs rooted in her father's rejection of Kathy's faith, we fell in love and were married. As I got to know Kathy's dad, Dennis, we developed a relationship that was first competitive, then tolerant, and ultimately filled with love and mutual respect. Over the first seven years of our marriage, Dennis came to accept Kathy's conversion and enthusiastically returned to our lives, welcoming his first grandson with much love and finding gentle, genuine ways to express his care and support. I never thought I'd hear him call me son, but in time he did, even listening intently and with questions as we had sought to share with him the love of Christ.

It was hard for the family when we moved to Chicago to attend seminary in 1986, but Dennis accepted it, as a big supporter of education. Even when we remained to start a church, he would often call and visit, and we were very thankful for his many kindnesses.

By 1990 and by God's grace, Kathy had much to be thankful for—a husband, two healthy baby boys, a newborn girl only six weeks old, and an exciting new church we had started together. She had a restored relationship with her father and an eternal relationship with her heavenly Father. Sovereignty was sweet.

In the summer of 1990, I planned to spend two weeks in Denver to begin my doctoral studies. My family had just visited our parents in Canada and had even shared the gospel with a more receptive Dennis than we had previously seen. I can still see him walking out the patio door—no shirt, deeply tanned in just shorts and sandals with the truth of the gospel ringing in his ears. We returned to Chicago rejoicing and praying that the seeds of truth would soon sprout into personal faith in Dennis's heart, and I boarded the plane for Denver.

Late that week Kathy called with the tone of voice every devoted husband dreads to hear. "James, there's been an accident. Dad has fallen off a roof during construction and . . . he's dead." I cannot recall the exact words spoken, but I remember the empty feeling of being so far from the one I longed to embrace. She boarded a plane for Canada with three preschoolers and returned to a grieving family with so much sorrow and so little hope.

We got through the funeral. I gave the gospel to the sneers of a sin-hardened crowd and stood with Kathy and our kids as the casket was *lowered into the ground. We endured the ritual of his pagan friends pour-ing beer on the grave site, the very substance that caused his unstable con-dition and fatal fall. As soon as we could, we loaded the kids into the car and headed back to Chicago with broken hearts and a lot of questions . . . about sovereignty.*

"But Lord, he was so close." "Clearly You were ripening his heart to the gospel." "Did he cry out for salvation in his last moments?" "Was he even now so loved and longed for in the horror of hell?" What loving heart can comprehend what sovereignty allows?

Weeks became months, and shock became sorrow deep and wide. Ques-tions would not yield to explanation. Comfort seemed selfish, and sover-eignty loomed largest of all as the only place of refuge. How well I remember the words that Kathy said after many months of puzzling: "I only want what God wants. I pray Dad's in heaven. I hope, like the thief on the cross, that he cried out for mercy, but most of all I know, 'shall not the Judge of all the earth deal justly?'" (Genesis 18:25). *To come trembling to the place where you bow the wounded heart and confess with much travail, "There is a God; He sovereignly rules the universe and does what is right. I often do not see or understand His ways, but I choose to trust Him. Someday I will know and see that He does all things well."*

Like it was yesterday I can hear my wife saying through her tears, "If my father cannot be in heaven because God has willed it so, then I don't want it either. I want to love God so much that I trust His every decision no mat-ter how hard that may be."

Is there sorrow? Yes, still there is sorrow, but it is surrounded by sover-eignty. Only faith can get you to the feet of sovereignty, and only grace can keep you there. If you are struggling to get there today, journey on, because no one arrives at this destination quickly or easily. However, don't let that dissuade you. It's a place of depth and quiet rest, one only comprehended when we can say from life's deepest valleys, "It happened to me."

GOD'S SOVEREIGNTY CELEBRATED

And because God is sovereign, He is able to do exactly as He pleas-es. What He pleases for you is to know Him through all the experi-ences of your life now, and someday, in the fullness of joy that only eternity can reveal. If that truth does not comfort you, it is because you are still fighting a war you can never win. God is sovereign, and there is incredible comfort in embracing what He chooses to allow, even when—no, *especially* when—that is most difficult for you. Someday we will stand with saints from every age of history and worship God for who He is—the righteous Ruler and the sovereign Lord. In that day we will overflow with joy at the infinite wisdom and immeasurable splendor of all that God has chosen and performed. **"For from Him and through Him and to Him are all things"** (Romans 11:36).

When you embrace that fully in the deepest part of who you are, only then do you know what it means to be gripped by the sovereignty of God. Make the choice now to bow in submission before the Sovereign. As you do that genuinely from your heart, you will be gripped by truly knowing (in a way that seeing could never accomplish) that God's sovereign purposes will ultimately prove loving and good.

LET'S PRAY

Sovereign God,

We thank You by faith for something we don't completely understand. Thank You for being in control of all. Others who have gone through valleys like I am facing have testified to Your faithfulness. I ask for Your grace as I choose by faith to take my eyes off my experience and wait in hope to see Your sovereign purposes revealed. Whether in this life or in the life to come, I am believing that You are good and do all things well. At times I don't see it, and even now I don't feel it, but I will not let those things rule my faith. You are good; generations have "tasted and seen that the Lord is good." I believe Your Word, and by faith I submit to Your sovereignty. Father, You are good. Lord, You are faithful.

I trust You. I submit to You. I worship You. In the name of Jesus I pray.

—*Amen.*

MAKE IT PERSONAL

- Do you tremble at God's Word? Are you worried that obedience to Scripture will be overwhelming? Too costly? What God-directed change are you resisting right now? Are you willing to change? If your honest answer to this final question is no, then ask God to make you *willing* to follow His way. You'll be amazed that someday soon your heart will begin to say, "You have the right to reign over me. I will go where You tell me, do what You ask. Because You are in control."

- On a piece of paper, write this declaration, date it, sign it, and keep it in your Bible:

  > I'm done resisting God.
  > I'm not going to fight Him anymore.
  > I'm not going to run from Him.
  > I'm not going to turn to my own way of thinking, rationalizing, or manipulating the circumstances.
  > I am going to embrace this situation as from the hand of a sovereign and loving God.
  > I am going to trust that He knows what He is doing . . . in my life, in the lives of those I love, and in the world.

- Being gripped by God's sovereignty doesn't take away your questions . . . but it will take away your anxiety. Determine today to surrender your *why?* questions to God. From your will, release God to resolve or not resolve any issue that looms large in your life. Ask God to make this a turning point in your lifelong walk with Him. Live with the mystery of how He is working all things together for your good even when you cannot see it or even imagine how. (See Romans 8:28 and Ephesians 1:11–12.)

- Being gripped by God's sovereignty also declares war on human pride. When you ask God to reveal His greatness, you will be overwhelmed with the miniature you compared to infinity itself. Respond with humility and glad surrender to the righteous ruler of the universe.

- Expression is an important part of the learning process. Share with a friend or family member what you are learning about God's greatness in this study. Your expression will encourage you both.

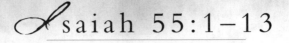

"Ho! Every one who thirsts, come to the waters;
And you who have no money come, buy and eat.
Come, buy wine and milk
Without money and without cost.
Why do you spend money for what is not bread,
And your wages for what does not satisfy?
Listen carefully to Me, and eat what is good,
And delight yourself in abundance.
Incline your ear and come to Me.
Listen, that you may live;
And I will make an everlasting covenant with you,
According to the faithful mercies shown to David.
Behold, I have made him a witness to the peoples,
A leader and commander for the peoples.
Behold, you will call a nation you do not know,
And a nation which knows you not will run to you,
Because of the LORD your God, even the Holy One of Israel;
For He has glorified you."
Seek the LORD while He may be found;
Call upon Him while He is near.
Let the wicked forsake his way
And the unrighteous man his thoughts;
And let him return to the LORD,
And He will have compassion on him,
And to our God,
For He will abundantly pardon.
"For My thoughts are not your thoughts,
Nor are your ways My ways," declares the LORD.
"For as the heavens are higher than the earth,
So are My ways higher than your ways
And My thoughts than your thoughts.
For as the rain and the snow come down from heaven,
And do not return there without watering the earth
And making it bear and sprout,
And furnishing seed to the sower and bread to the eater;
So will My word be which goes forth from My mouth;
It will not return to Me empty,
Without accomplishing what I desire,
And without succeeding in the matter for which I sent it.
For you will go out with joy

And be led forth with peace;
The mountains and the hills will break forth into shouts of joy before you,
And all the trees of the field will clap their hands.
Instead of the thorn bush the cypress will come up,
And instead of the nettle the myrtle will come up,
And it will be a memorial to the LORD,
For an everlasting sign which will not be cut off."

Stop and look; observe the incredible work
that God is doing in this world. Find your
highest joy and deepest satisfaction by
entering into that work.

Chapter Four

GRIPPED
by the
WORKS
of GOD

Isaiah 55:1–13

ONE OF THE DARKEST PLACES in my Christian experience is the grief I feel over Christians who quit—especially leaders I know who used to be in the race and stretching for the tape with their whole hearts. What happened, and why did they pack it in?

I've heard it said that the crises of life reveal something that has been happening for a long time. In the case of AWOL (that's military for "absent without leave") Christians, I believe that is true. We tend to focus on the shock of the tire blowing out, but in reality there were a lot of maintenance issues that preceded the flashing lights and the flares by the side of the highway. Somewhere, much earlier on, they lost their longing for God.

I must confess that the fear of following in their footsteps sometimes haunts me. Do you know what I mean? I sure don't want to crawl across the finish line a defeated, derailed Christian, or worse—give up the race before the final stretch even starts. No, I would guess that like me you want to break that tape with arms high and your face toward the sun and say with the apostle Paul, **"I have finished the course, I have kept the faith"** (2 Timothy 4:7).

So let's not pretend. There is in every human heart a propensity "to leave the God we love" unless we are continually gripped by His greatness, unless on a regular basis we allow our hearts and minds to be rocked with the truth of all that He is.

That's one reason I love to be around faithful men and women who have followed after the greatness of God for half a century or more.

Like Roy.

Roy and his wife, Carol, were among the eighteen people whom God first gave a vision for the church that would become Harvest Bible Chapel. I remember when Roy talked with me about pastoring this soon-to-be church. He had a passion for the things of God like few men his age (he was then sixty-one). This past fall Harvest celebrated sixteen years of ministry, and you could still find Roy serving and singing, still fired up about God's Word. His hair has thinned a bit, his health faltered, but there's a flash in his eyes as he talks about what he currently sees God doing. *Currently* sees. God still draws his heart like a magnet. And on any given Sunday, people still line up to pray with him after every service. Why? Because it's obvious Roy is gripped by God's greatness.

WHY WALK WITH GOD?

Attractive? Yeah, for me too. And that's the kind of life Isaiah spreads out in front of us in chapter 55. In beautiful detail, he describes the benefits of walking with God over the long haul. They are:

- *Permanent* and *complete satisfaction* with the things of God.
- Abundance this world knows nothing about.
- Immeasurable forgiveness—that transforms your heart and transfers to others.
- Truth that takes root in your life and produces a bumper crop of "God confidence," year after year.

These are the works of God that keep people's hearts beating after Him for fifty, sixty, or seventy years. And it's all in Isaiah 55.

Nowhere else in the Bible do we read a chapter packed more fully with God's invitation to personally experience His works. Only here can we read such conviction about God's great deeds designed before the foundation of the world. Nothing can stop Him. You might as well try to keep the rain from falling.

"God is great!" Isaiah says. "His truth will accomplish whatever God wants just as surely as the rain will come in spring to water the dry and thirsty earth" (see v. 10).

Isaiah 55: An Invitation to Experience God's Works

Is that the kind of refreshment you need for your marathon in God? C'mon, run alongside me for a while; I want to show you the phenomenal work that God is doing—not just a long time ago, but in our world today and potentially in our hearts in the next few minutes. It's time to be gripped by the works of God.

There are at least fifty different lessons to be learned in the thirteen verses of Isaiah 55. All of them relate in some way to the fullness, excellence, and everlasting blessing of recognizing and reveling in all that God is doing. Like spokes in a wheel, each points to the God whose works continually invite our worship. Isaiah 55 is an open invitation to experience God's works. So let's jump in!

In God We Find Abundant Satisfaction. "Ho! Every one who thirsts, come to the waters." (v. 1)

I know something about you. You are like me. You are like all of the people whom God has created and placed on this earth. You're thirsty for God. He has built within each of us a need that only He can satisfy. Isaiah longs for God's people to "get it"—to understand everything that His promise of satisfaction can mean to them.

Look at that first word, **"Ho!"** Isaiah is trying to get your attention before he makes a massive assertion.

So, OK, you've got my attention. What's the point?

The point is that God wants to be for your soul what water is for your body. If you've ever been dehydrated from heavy work in the hot sun, you know that milk, Diet Pepsi, Gatorade, or whatever—they just don't cut it. When you're really thirsty, nothing satisfies like water.

We take water for granted, but in Isaiah's day you couldn't just turn on the tap for a drink. Fresh, pure, clean water was an incredible resource. Like a water boy after football practice in the hot Texas sun, Isaiah shouts, "Come and get it!"

So why doesn't everyone drink?

Objection #1

"That sounds really good, but I can't afford that water." Doesn't matter, Isaiah says; come anyway. Hear me on this one: Nothing that God wants to give you will ever cost you a thin dime. You think you can't afford God's gift? You're right. Good thing everything God gives is "on Him." Everything! The next time somebody tells you that you have to do something to deserve what God offers you, call it for what it is—a lie!

> Everything that God wants to give to you is free.

In fact, think about it. What's the biggest insult you can give someone who gives you a gift? Suppose your mom buys you a Christmas present. She's so excited to put this beautifully wrapped present in your hands, and you get out your wallet and insist on reimbursing her. What an insult! Same thing for God. Eternity isn't long enough to pay for what God has done for us; that's why it comes as a gift.

Objection #2

"Sure, water is great and everything, but I need more than water." What?!

"No, really I do. The Bible and church—that's all great stuff. But I need more than that." Have you ever said in your heart that God was not enough to satisfy you?

Isaiah asserts, "And you who have no money come, buy and eat. Come, buy wine and milk without money and without cost."

The text says that God is like wine and milk. The word *eat* implies food. Not only will God satisfy our thirst with water, but He has also prepared the greatest banquet ever served to feed our hungry souls. Notice who's invited—the thirsty and the penniless, those who totally admit their need for God. Do you admit your need? If so you are invited too.

A LESSON IN SATISFACTION

Let's play "Name that Person."

➤ Born July 26, 1943, in Dartford, Kent, England
➤ Met Keith Richards as a five-year-old schoolmate
➤ Years later formed a band and performed around London as "The Rolling Stones"
➤ Propelled to the top of the charts in the United States with one song recognized as an "all-time great."
➤ A life strewn with drug arrests, illegitimate children, and riotous concerts that resulted in multiple deaths

Can you guess the name that belongs to this tragic life? Trade magazines herald him as one of rock 'n' roll's great successes, yet the emptiness of Mick Jagger's life calls out pathetically like one of his hit songs, "I Can't Get No Satisfaction."

Mick Jagger said in one interview, "I would rather be dead than singing 'Satisfaction' at [age] 45." In 2005, he turns sixty-two and continues the sad refrain. It's not like he hasn't searched for satisfaction, but like so many, he is ever searching and **"never able to come to the knowledge of the truth"** (2 Timothy 3:7). God promises water to quench people's eternal thirst, yet they have chosen a path that leaves them eating sand.

Do you get it? The only way you can know satisfaction in life is in a deep and fulfilling relationship with God. If you have never turned to Him, what else can I say to make you see the eternal significance of your choice? If you have been living apart from Him and trying to fill that emptiness in your life with other things, please—stop! Come to Him and discover the satisfaction that God alone can bring.

If you have experienced this, you're probably saying, "Right on!" Experiencing the greatness of God is like a satisfying meal to the starving. Like a drink of cold water to a man in the desert. The psalmist agreed when he wrote: **"Oh give thanks to the LORD, for He is good, . . . for He has satisfied the thirsty soul, and the hungry soul He has filled with what is good"** (Psalm 107:1, 9).

Isaiah 55 equals "God is enough." And once you experience the real thing, you'll never long for anything else. He will satisfy you with *all* that He is. Are you in?

GET A GRIP ON GOD'S GREATNESS
God's Renewable Grace

> *G*od is the ultimate promise keeper. His name *Jehovah* reminds us that He is totally committed to humankind. He's a covenant keeping God. A covenant is like a turbo promise; it's very official and clearly understood by all. God's works in Isaiah 55 all find their root in His character trait *hesed*—meaning His covenant love, His mercy and steadfast lovingkindness. Because of His *hesed*, He satisfies you with His kindness. He forgives you in His mercy. His life in you brings absolute delight. Not that you or anyone deserves it . . . but God's *hesed* (which Lamentations 3:23 promises is new every morning) is the Old Testament equivalent of *grace*. Being gripped by God's works is to be gripped by *hesed*, God's covenantal love.

A RELATIONSHIP THAT WILL LAST FOREVER
"I WILL MAKE AN EVERLASTING COVENANT WITH YOU." (V. 3)

It might surprise you, but a covenant is not a *contract*. A contract involves two people who agree to perform in a certain way. "I'll do this . . . you do that." If either party reneges on their part, the contract is broken.

When the Bible reveals God as a covenant God, this means God has entered into a relationship that cannot be changed by our behavior. If God were a contract God, then when we acted incorrectly or lived sinfully, the contract would be broken. But a covenant is a relationship that is not dependent on the performance of one of the parties. All the responsibility lies on one side. God says, "I'm making a covenant commitment to you. I'm entering into a relationship with you that you can't mess up in any way." Sounds really permanent, doesn't it?

You may wonder what that relationship will look like. Isaiah tells us. "It's going to be like God's relationship with David." That's the illustration God chose to describe the relationship He wants to have with us: **"I will make an everlasting covenant with you, according to the faithful mercies shown to David."**

Do you remember David? That guy's whole life was mercy.

- ➤ First, a lion tried to kill him; God spared the shepherd boy. (1 Samuel 17:34–37)
- ➤ Then a bear tried to kill him; God saved him again.
- ➤ Then there was that whole giant thing with Goliath.
- ➤ Then crazy King Saul tried to kill David—chased him all over the country shouting "Murder him!" Again and again, God protected David. (1 Samuel 24)
- ➤ Then God put David on the throne of Israel, and everything was great until the Bathsheba scandal. But even adultery and murder couldn't stop God's mercy from flowing into David's life from this covenant God. (Psalm 51)

David is the poster boy for what God means by covenantal relationship. You may at times wish God would be as generous with you. Fact is, He will because He promises to measure His kindness **"according to the mercies shown to David."**

But It's Even Bigger than That!

Hold on, God says. My mercy is even bigger than that!

Get this: God says through Isaiah, **"Behold, you will call a nation you do not know, and a nation which knows you not will** run to you, because of the LORD your God, even the Holy One of Israel; for He has glorified you" (v. 5).

My salvation, God says, is not just about one nation anymore . . . it's about the whole earth. What began as a specific plan for one specific people, God is spreading across the globe. God is drawing people to Himself in every country on the face of the earth. That's more than three hundred nations. No time zones, borders, cultures, or languages can hinder God's works from being known. He is great—nothing can hold Him back! God says in verses 4 and 5, "This thing is going to get really big. I'm going to be pardoning people all over the place." How cool is that?

But you have to do your part!

Seek the LORD while He may be found; call upon Him while He is near. (v. 6)

God is taking people who will seek Him and call upon Him. But notice the urgency of the matter. Scripture says, today is the day of salvation. Notice what it says: **"Seek the Lord while He may be found; call upon Him while He is *near*"** (emphasis added). That implies that the hour of conviction must be the hour of decision.

Is God pricking your heart about His greatness today? Whether you need to return to Him or call upon Him for the very first time by faith, you need to make that decision right now. Not next Friday; not a month from today; the hour of conviction has to be the hour of decision. Why? Because Genesis 6:3 says that the Spirit of God will not always strive with men. You don't know if you're going to be alive next Friday. You don't know if you're going to be in your right mind next Friday or if the grace of God is going to be working and stirring your heart next Friday. You don't know if you have time. If God is dealing with your heart right now, you need to respond right now! Respond to Him today and experience the pardon.

You say, "I want to do that. How do I do that?"

Look at verse 7: **"Let the wicked forsake his way."** Now, if you're still at the place where you're offended about being called *wicked,* then you have some work to do. Those of us who have found the Lord understand that we have all failed Him. We say, in effect, "You know what? My life was so wrong and so lame! It was going nowhere, but I have turned from that sin, and now I'm living for Him with my whole heart!" That's how you get to the Lord. You have to forsake those wicked ways. Then notice the next phrase, **"and the unrighteous man his thoughts."** That's where it all begins, isn't it? In our thoughts. Wrong thinking leads to wrong living.

"And let him return to the LORD." Forsake and return. Those are Old Testament terms for repentance and faith. "Return to the Lord." Why? Because we can't earn our own forgiveness; it is only by faith in what the Lord has done for us that our sins can be forgiven.

Maybe you've known the Lord for many years, but your heart is not close to the Lord. Well, it works the same way—forsake and return. Leave what anchors your heart to the emptiness of this world, and return to God as your passion and priority.

What's holding you back?

What keeps you from returning to the Lord? I think a big issue that many face is "What kind of reception am I going to get?" That was on the mind of the guy in Luke 15, the prodigal son, who lived like a fool, far from home and father. If you know Jesus' story, don't allow its familiarity to steal the point. We'll pick it up halfway through.

The son (a picture of us) was living far from home and far from the life he knew he should live. He had turned his back on his father (a picture of God). One day he woke up and said, "Am I crazy or what? What am I doing over here eating slop and living like a pig?" He said, "I'm going to return to my father. I'm going home."

Although the son had walked away from his father, his father never stopped looking for him. When the son came to his senses, he did the "self-talk" thing all the way home. *How will Dad receive me? How can I make up for what I've done? What kind of reception am I going to get?* He was worried.

Have you worried like that?

Perhaps you can relate. You ask, "What kind of response am I going to get if I return to the Lord?" I've watched people picture God in one of three ways:

1. *Some people picture God as an angry God.* They think to themselves, "When I return to the Lord, He's going to stand there and say, 'Do you think you can live the way you've been living and just come waltzing back in here and everything will be all fine and dandy? Well, you're wrong!'" No! God is not going to think or feel that way toward you. Maybe your dad or mom was like that, but God isn't. When we return to the Lord, He welcomes us back in love. I'll show you His actual response a little later in the chapter.

2. *Some people picture God as an anxious God.* He's like, "Where have you been? We've been worried sick about you. We were wondering if you were ever going to come back! You've had us up half the night!" What a foolish notion—as if God were ever worried about anything!

3. *Some people picture God as an ambivalent God.* You come into the room and He barely looks up from the newspaper. "Oh, you're back. Fine. Throw your things in the corner, and don't bother Me; I'm busy." Again, that is so not God's heart.

In his wildest imagination, the runaway son never would have dreamt what his father did next. When the father saw him coming down the road, he got up and *ran* toward him. It's the only time in all of Scripture that God is pictured as running. The father didn't just wait for him—he ran to him according to Luke 15:20 and threw his arms around him and fell on his neck and kissed him. Do you see why God put that in His Word? When we are convicted of our sin and we sense our need to return to the Lord, we won't ever have to wonder, "What kind of reception am I going to get?"

Long ago, Isaiah recorded what you can expect to get from God today. When you turn back to Him, you'll see Him running toward you. He longs to embrace you, Isaiah writes: **"And He will have compassion on him, and to our God, for He will abundantly pardon"** (v. 7). What a phenomenal promise.

One of my privileges as a pastor is to hear real-life stories of modern prodigals. I'm still fired up from a recent weekend when we got to hear repeated accounts of God's work in people's lives. We heard 254 life stories in all, as these 254 joyous, awe-struck people were baptized. It was a great weekend of victory.

Here's what's interesting—they all told the same story. Now, if you were there you might say, "No—their stories were different." Yes, but in a deeper way they were the same. Every life had the same theme: "I was going along, thinking I was too sexy for my shirt . . . and then God dropped a boulder on my life." By boulder I mean some crushing personal experience that obliterates pride and independence from God. The only thing different in their real-life accounts was the specific label on the boulder. For some it was a marriage crisis; others experienced a health or financial burden that caused great anxiety. Still others reported a penetrating loneliness or a profound loss that they just couldn't shake.

Then came God! They went on to report with different words but total unanimity that when they did turn to Him, they discovered that God wasn't just a bunch of information. They experienced His forgiveness in a profound and life-altering way.

That's a picture of abundant pardon.

A NEW LOOK AT FORGIVENESS

I have a confession to make. For most of my ministry, I've taught this passage out of context. (Gasp!) In fact, I see now that the way I've always understood it missed the exciting fullness that God intended. Look at it:

> *"For My thoughts are not your thoughts, neither are your ways My ways," declares the LORD. "For as the heavens are higher than the earth, so are My ways higher than your ways and My thoughts than your thoughts."* (vv. 8–9)

I've always believed this passage taught that God is not like us; God is bigger than us. Even though that's true, that's not the primary point. Look at the context.

God is like, "Let's get something straight right now. When y'all think about forgiveness, your thoughts are so different than Mine. When people sin against you, your way of handling it is so completely different than the way I handle it when people sin against Me."

So, how different are our thoughts than God's thoughts about forgiveness? They're polar opposites.

Think about your greatest concept of forgiveness or the most abundant pardon you could imagine. Right now, think of your biggest thing. What would be the greatest offense for which you could ever forgive someone? Got it? OK, now go lower. Are you there? Imagine, for example, a sin that would involve the greatest sin against the most wonderful person perpetrated by the lowest and most vile sinner. What comes to your mind? Think of Saddam Hussein or Adolf Hitler and the countless innocents they tortured and murdered. Think of the forgiveness it would take to erase all that they did.

In what ways are God's thoughts bigger than our thoughts? Answer: when He forgives.

Now go deeper still, to something even worse, even harder to forgive. Get your ugliest and most awful offense clearly in mind and imagine the amount of forgiveness necessary to get that done. Got it?

Without even knowing your thoughts, I'll tell you the result—your greatest concept of forgiveness (mine, too) is pretty weak compared to God's thoughts. We're not even close. God says, **"For as the heavens are higher than the earth . . ."** (v. 9).

Here's how we measure forgiveness:

1. *We think about* who. Who should we forgive? "She did this and I don't know if I could forgive her." We think about the people involved. Do we really want to forgive *them*? We measure their value and question if they are worthy of our forgiveness.

2. *We think about* how much. We say to some things on our list, "No problem, I can forgive that." But sometimes we put our foot down and say, "Hey, that's a bigger thing! I can't forgive *that!*" So we think about who it is; we keep track of how much they've done.

3. *We think about* how often. How's that saying go? "Fool me once, shame on you. Fool me twice, shame on me." We're like, "*Nobody's*

going to do that to me again!" We measure everything. We measure who did it, how big the offense was, and how often we were victimized.

4. *We think about* how many people. "If one person does it, I can let it go. But everybody has been running all over me; I have to put a stop to this!" We measure forgiveness with precision and puny capacity. I wonder if God shakes His head and says, "Your thoughts are so lame. They're so little. Look at Me and get the bigger picture."

THE BIGGER PICTURE OF FORGIVENESS

We can't conceive God's boundaries on forgiveness. They're so much bigger and different than we can get into our heads. Anybody who says that they can explain God's forgiveness is minimizing Scripture. Even God says, "You haven't come close to getting My thing on pardon. It's so totally different from yours."

A man with a hundred billion dollars does not need to count pennies. So God, who is infinitely wealthy in forgiveness, doesn't measure or count it in any way. Think for a moment of all of the people in all of human history and all of the forgiveness that God has granted to all of the people. Can our minds even go that far? And since all of our sin is ultimately against God, imagine all the times He has chosen to forgive. Isaiah is right—as high as the heavens are above the earth . . . and then double it . . . and again, *ad infinitum*.

Charles Spurgeon said, "God's pardon is abundant because it wells up from an infinitely deep fountain. Our sins may pile as high as the tallest mountains, but Jesus' blood, like Noah's flood, drowns them all." Now that's abundant pardon.

This is all great in theory, but now I'm going to meddle. Are you thinking, "God could *never* forgive my thing. If I ever really brought my sin before the Lord, He would turn His back. I'm just going to have to carry this one myself because He's just not merciful enough to forgive me." My friend, you are *so* wrong! God can completely forgive everything. That's the whole point of God's greatness—His is a level of grace and forgiveness called abundant pardon that we struggle to comprehend.

But wait. Abundant pardon is not yours simply because it's been offered. It must be received and accepted. Perhaps you have never made the choice to claim God's forgiveness. You've seen others' lives changed, but your life hasn't changed . . . why? Because you have never received God's abundant pardon.

In 1826, two men, last names Porter and Wilson, were sentenced to hang for robbing the US Postal Service. Porter was hanged first in July 1830. Three weeks later, President Andrew Jackson pardoned Wilson, the second perpetrator. The death sentence was lifted.

Then the weirdest thing happened. Wilson refused the pardon, "I don't want the forgiveness." How bizarre! It sent the court system into confusion. *What do we do? The president has pardoned him, and he doesn't want to be forgiven.* The case took three years to resolve. It even went to the Supreme Court, where Justice John Marshall passed down an historic decision regarding the acceptance or rejection of a pardon. Here is what the Supreme Court said:

"Pardon is an act of grace which exempts the individual on whom it is bestowed from the punishment of the law. A pardon is a deed to the validity of which delivery is essential. Delivery is not complete without acceptance. It then may be rejected by the person to whom it is rendered. If the pardon is rejected, we have found no power in the Court to force it upon him."

Do you get how perfectly that parallels God's law? It doesn't matter how ready God is to pardon you if you will not accept it personally. If you will not embrace what God offers freely, if you won't by faith receive God's forgiveness, then He won't force it on you.

But to you who grasp the weight of the death sentence that our own sin truly deserves and then choose to be set free, you *know* what it's like to be gripped by the greatness of God! And you're smiling right now because you know to whom all the credit goes. And the glory. Because God is good.

As King David said, **"Forget none of His benefits; who pardons all your iniquities . . . who redeems your life from the pit, who crowns you with lovingkindness and compassion; who satisfies your years with good things"** (Psalm 103:2–5).

That's not only abundant pardon; that's amazing grace. Stop! Ponder the greatness of that forgiveness and let it grip you before you move on. Picture yourself awash in the sea of God's forgiveness—so unworthy but so abundantly pardoned. It's God's work, and it is truly great; let it grip your heart right now!

IN GOD'S WORD
WE FIND ACCOMPLISHED TRUTH

Understood only in the last few hundred years by scientists but here written several thousands of years ago, the natural water cycle is explained in Isaiah 55:10–11. (Don't you *love* God's Word?) Rainwater doesn't just come down; it goes up again. God says, "My rain never comes down without accomplishing in the earth the purpose for which I send it down."

In the very same sense, God says, "My Word never comes down and returns without performing the job I intended it to do." Every time a mother or father or pastor or small-group leader or children's ministry worker speaks the Word of God, God says, "You think you're speaking, but what is really happening is that I'm sending forth My Word."

I just love verses 10 and 11. Picture the scene:

"For as the rain and the snow come down from heaven, and do not return there without watering the earth and making it bear and sprout, and furnishing seed to the sower and bread to the eater; so will My word be which goes forth from My mouth; it will not return to Me empty, without accomplishing what I desire, and without succeeding in the matter for which I sent it."

Rain keeps us alive: It waters the earth and germinates seed, which produces bread to the eater—sustenance and nourishment. But as good as that is, God's Word has an even better promise of return. "My Word will not return to Me empty." That's a 100 percent promise: *Never* will the Word of God go forth but that it will bear fruit. That is the work of God—so great in its extent that it can only grip our hearts in wonder. Everywhere around the world at this moment where God's Word is going forth, it has God's guarantee going with it. Something good is going to happen.

Parents, are you sowing the seed of God's Word into the hearts of your kids? God says, "Every time you sow that seed into the life of your child, it's going to bear fruit."

You say, "But I go through days of doubting and weeks of wondering. I live and quote and memorize Scripture till they think I'm a walking Bible, and I just haven't see the results." Listen. God says, "Don't worry about *your* part in that; I'm going to honor My Word."

> If you sow the seed of God's Word into people's lives, God promises that He will accomplish what He desires to accomplish.

What would we talk about if we didn't talk about the Bible? What on earth would your pastor have to say to you? Nothing. Weather reports? Book reviews? We've got our noses in the book God wrote right now as we study Isaiah. God says, "Every time you open the pages of My Word and you speak My truth, I'm going to make sure it bears fruit." That's the only confidence that keeps me preaching every single week.

I'll let you in on a pastor's secret. Sometimes we pastors get really, really tired of standing up with an open Bible in front of people with closed hearts. So why do we do it? The reason is right here in verses 10 and 11. You've got to circle this one in your Bible.

God's holy Word will always get results. God's commitment to His Word is one of His greatest works.

Maybe you're sharing Christ with someone at work or in your neighborhood. Maybe you're burdened for someone you love. Sow the seed of God's Word in his or her life. Drop your dependence on human persuasion. Lose the platitude, "Well, I'm keeping the doors open and trying not to offend." Their salvation has nothing to do with whether they *like* you. Sow the seed of God's Word. Scatter the seed, and wait for the fruit. Drop all your clever arguments and persuasions and share the Word of God.

Are you discouraged? Get alone today and open the book of Psalms and read God's Word back to Him. If you're facing temptation, read Matthew 4. When Jesus faced temptation, He said, **"It is written . . . It is written . . . It is written"** (vv. 4, 7, 10). God makes an incredible promise about the power of His work through His Word.

STAY FAITHFUL

I struggled spiritually when I was in high school. I can remember a time when I had just returned to the Lord and was trying to get my life back together. My youth pastor *made* me go to this conference. I didn't want to go, but looking back I see now God was drawing me back to Himself.

The conference speaker was Tom Maharias from Manhattan Bible Church. He shared from Scripture why it was impossible for the character of Christ to grow in the life of a person whose mind was filled with worldly sewage. That was me. What I told you earlier about the Rolling Stones, I knew very personally because my whole life was polluted by the heavy-metal filth I poured through my headphones in daily doses.

> Be faithful to sow the truth of His Word, and He promises that it will not return without succeeding in the purpose for which He sent it forth. It's one of God's greatest works.

But now I had returned to the Lord. I was trying to go forward spiritually, but I was chained to something that was holding me back. Pastor Maharias challenged us with "Do you want the character of Christ to grow in your mind? Then get the sewage out." He wisely pressed us to make a decision. He challenged us to stand up and make a public consecrated decision to put only Christ-honoring messages in our minds.

It was one of those times when I just knew that the Lord was speaking to me, so I stood up. I remember my body felt like lead. Out of several hundred young people, I was the only person to stand that day. The only one.

Twenty years later, I had the opportunity to meet Tom Maharias. I asked if he remembered the teen conference in Ontario, Canada. He said, "I remember that well. I was so discouraged. I preached my heart out and went home wondering if God did a single thing that day."

I said, "That day changed my life!"

If you're weary in doing the right thing, stay at it. You can trust that as the rains come and go, God is at work behind the scenes . . . growing His fruit to be ready for harvest in His time.

FINDING ABSOLUTE
DELIGHT IN GOD'S WORKS

"For you will go out with joy and be led forth with peace; the mountains and the hills will break forth into shouts of joy before you, and all the trees of the field will clap their hands." (vv. 12–13)

Even on the sunniest day, everything looks dull and hazy when your eyes are closed to the reality of your Creator God. Looming over any delightful scene are the questions, "Where is all of this going? What's the purpose of all of this?"

But when your eyes are opened to the greatness of God's works, suddenly you hear birds singing and everything becomes beautiful. God's created world bursts into praise before your eyes! Suddenly your overwhelming desire is to join nature's chorus of worship to God! It's not just the trees and mountains that acknowledge the reality of their Designer. As the pinnacle of God's creation, we're supposed to be leading the band.

That's what verse 13 talks about. **"Instead of the thorn bush** [thorns were part of the curse in Genesis 3] **the cypress will come up** [a strong, useful life is pictured in that tree], **and instead of the nettle the myrtle will come up, and it will be a memorial to the LORD."** Isaiah says your life is a memorial to God. Your life is a testimony to the faithfulness and the greatness of God, **"an everlasting sign which will not be cut off"** (v. 13).

The picture here is of pure delight in God. "Listen carefully to Me, and eat what is good, and delight yourself in abundance." Hear that? Delight yourself in the great things of God! Enjoy them. Open your heart to what He's doing. Don't be afraid to look and laugh and love God's wonderful work.

It Happened to Me

ROY

Remember my friend Roy? (I told you about him at the beginning of this chapter.) Roy exemplifies what I was just challenging you about—he loved and laughed and reveled in God's wonderful work his whole life. It kept him in the race and on course.

Just a few weeks ago the phone rang at home, and it was Rick, our associate senior pastor, who focuses his energies on congregational care. I could tell by the sound of his voice that something was wrong, and as he took a deep breath, I found myself doing the same.

"James, I am over at Roy's . . ." he began, "and just a few moments ago he went to be with the Lord."

Time stood still in that moment as my mind flooded with a thousand memories. Gone, just like that. In a split second, Roy was gone from this life and entered the next.

Normally at such a critical moment, I would have leapt from my chair and rushed to the side of the grieving. But this was different; I was the one who was grieving the loss of a dear friend and fellow leader—a rock in the life of our church. I needed some time to gather myself before the Lord or I would not have anything to give others. I sat in that chair for over an hour, my kids coming and going, the television droning in the background, and my mind far away, reviewing the record of Roy's life, so well lived, so deeply steeped in the experience and observation of God's works.

Roy was truly a founder in our church. When we lost some founding members to division and needless separation, Roy was the strength that brought us to Christ and held us all together. Roy was the thermostat for this young pastor so prone to overheating. He had the ability to calm my troubled soul and get me back on task, showing me how to trust God, how to wait on God, and always, always showing me grace and forgiveness.

He was number one at welcoming others and the force that found and fed our few seniors. Roy was quick to laugh and slow to judge. He was easily grieved by harshness or haughtiness. Roy was the visionary who found our first church property and followed my leadership even when the future was uncertain. He was a man who was gripped by the works of God.

Not surprisingly, his wake was standing room only. Fifty yards of mourners lined the church lobby for hours waiting for a chance to repeat the refrain: "God worked in my life through Roy . . ." The hours raced by, and the stories never got old. The funeral was a celebration. Children and grandchildren stood through their tears and rehearsed their own experience of God at work through Roy.

I'm telling you, there is no life better than this. Roy had been taken and shaken by God many years ago and, never ever let go.

Do you have that? Have you been gripped by the works of God? Have you experienced His satisfaction? His abundant pardon? The power of His Word penetrating your heart? Do you want to experience that again? Even now? Roy had this going on big-time, and you can too, but you must express yourself. You must! I know this for a fact . . . because it happened to me!

DON'T JUST THINK IT; EXPRESS YOURSELF!

Doing what I do, I go to more than my share of funerals. Over the years I've witnessed hundreds of people stand and give testimonies of the one whose life they are celebrating. I've come to realize that in their expressions of love, their grief is overshadowed by joy. C. S. Lewis had something important to say about this. He said that people don't have some incessant need to compliment, but that "people in love tell one another how beautiful they are because the joy is not complete without the expression."

Get that: "The joy is not complete without the expression." Until you say "I love you" and "I thank God for you" to the loved ones in your life, your joy cannot be complete. And it's the same with God. If you know the Lord, then throughout this chapter there has been something welling up inside of you saying, "Yes! God is the God of satisfaction and abundant pardon! Yes! His Word *does* accomplish the purpose for which it is sent forth. Yes! My only delight can be found in Him! His works are gripping, and I have to tell Him so."

I challenge you to do that today. You don't need a choir, guitar, or congregation to acknowledge the works of God in your world. The sky can be your stained-glass ceiling. If your heart is gripped by the greatness of God's work before your eyes, let your expression of praise be audible. And when it is . . . well, you'll see.

LET'S PRAY

Father,

Don't every let me forget Your incredible works in my life—works that bring me satisfaction, abundance, forgiveness, truth, and delight. Each one of them is gold. Keep me from embracing the temptation that anything apart from You could ever satisfy me. In the long, difficult days, restore my heart with the reminder of Your *hesed.* Prompt me with every sunrise to remember Your faithfulness, renewable for eternity. I want to be faithful back. Thank You for Your work in my life. Help me never to get over the greatness of Your works.

—Amen.

MAKE IT PERSONAL

1. Meditate on Psalm 63:1: **"O God, You are my God; I shall seek You earnestly; my soul thirsts for You, my flesh yearns for You, in a dry and weary land where there is no water."**

   What would it mean to you to want God as much as David, the psalmist, wanted Him?

2. Read over Isaiah 55:1–13. Choose a verse, phrase, or word from your reading and ponder it. Ask questions of it. Pray over it. Write it in your Bible study notebook, and look up other verses that use the same word. Look for at least one way you could apply it or live it. Linger over it. As you soak your soul slowly in the water of the Word, ask God to refresh you with it and prompt a satisfying thirst for more.

3. If you long after God—to want to know Him and please Him and to grow in spiritual maturity—that's the work of God's grace in your soul. Be thankful for it. In your carnal state (your life before you were a believer in Christ Jesus), this wouldn't have been your desire. But when a man thirsts after God, it proves that God's Spirit is alive and active within him, and he enjoys God's abundance (see Psalm 36:8 and Matthew 5:6). If you desire more of this, ask God to make you more thirsty for Him. Psalm 107:9 would be a great verse to memorize!

4. When you are gripped by the greatness of God's works, it fires you up to faithfulness. In fact, nothing is more essential to success in the Christian life than endurance . . . perseverance . . . keeping at it. Remembering God's work in your life will help you persevere.

   > God's works bring complete satisfaction. Ask yourself, "Will I get that anywhere else?"
   > God's works prompt His abundant pardon. "Who else promises forgiveness of sin?"
   > God's works provide accomplished truth. "Who else can accomplish everything he says he will?"
   > God's works produce absolute delight. "Is there anything else that can give me real joy?"

As you may already know, the answers to all these questions are found only in God. Stay faithful—it's worth it.

5. Seek out people in your family or church who have walked with God for more than fifty years. Invite them to coffee or to a meal, and ask them to share milestones of their spiritual journey. Be alert to the factors that have shaped their faithfulness, and build them into your own life. Look for a way to honor them for their model.

Observances of Fasts

"Cry loudly, do not hold back;
Raise your voice like a trumpet,
And declare to My people their transgression
And to the house of Jacob their sins.
Yet they seek Me day by day and delight to know My ways,
As a nation that has done righteousness
And has not forsaken the ordinance of their God.
They ask Me for just decisions,
They delight in the nearness of God.
'Why have we fasted and You do not see?
Why have we humbled ourselves and You do not notice?'
Behold, on the day of your fast you find your desire,
And drive hard all your workers.
Behold, you fast for contention and strife and to strike with a wicked fist.
You do not fast like you do today to make your voice heard on high.
Is it a fast like this which I choose, a day for a man to humble himself?
Is it for bowing one's head like a reed
And for spreading out sackcloth and ashes as a bed?
Will you call this a fast, even an acceptable day to the LORD?
Is this not the fast which I choose,
To loosen the bonds of wickedness,
To undo the bands of the yoke,
And to let the oppressed go free
And break every yoke?
Is it not to divide your bread with the hungry
And bring the homeless poor into the house;
When you see the naked, to cover him;
And not to hide yourself from your own flesh?
Then your light will break out like the dawn,
And your recovery will speedily spring forth;
And your righteousness will go before you;
The glory of the LORD will be your rear guard.
Then you will call, and the LORD will answer;
You will cry, and He will say, 'Here I am.'
If you remove the yoke from your midst,
The pointing of the finger and speaking wickedness,
And if you give yourself to the hungry
And satisfy the desire of the afflicted,
Then your light will rise in darkness

And your gloom will become like midday.
And the LORD will continually guide you,
And satisfy your desire in scorched places,
And give strength to your bones;
And you will be like a watered garden,
And like a spring of water whose waters do not fail."

God shows up powerfully when our

worship is sincere and fervent in spite of

whatever difficult circumstance we might

be experiencing.

Chapter Five

GRIPPED
by the
WORSHIP
of GOD

Isaiah 58:1–11

OK, YOU'VE READ THIS FAR, and that means you really want to be gripped by the reality of God's greatness. Perfect!

What we have discovered about God's greatness should and would grip you if you truly embrace it with your whole heart. But if you're a person who likes action, you may be saying to yourself, "Learning, learning, learning. Isn't there something for me *to do?*" Yes! In fact, if you worship the way this chapter explains, and I absolutely guarantee that almighty God will grip you with His greatness.

You say, "James, how can you possibly know what God will do for me?" Because I know what He has promised. In fact, I am so sure about this that I am going to press you very hard to take action—even if you feel you are already doing it. In this chapter, I am going to push you to get out of your comfort zone, and I don't care if that makes you mad. If you love someone, you have to be willing to risk the discomfort of pushing them toward something for their good. In fact, that's what God calls preachers to be all about. Consider then the passion God invited Isaiah to express on this all-important subject:

"Cry loudly, do not hold back; raise your voice like a trumpet, and declare to My people . . ." (v. 1)

In other words, Say it *now* and say it *loud!*

"Now, don't get so worked up," some people might say. "God's Word should be taught in a calm, cool, careful manner." Well, *forget-aboutit!* If the world can shout trash and trivia all day, certainly God's people can get fired up about what the Creator commands and calls us to. We don't have to hold back—we can lift God's Word so high that it leaps right off this page!

What's our message? Isaiah spells it out as chapter 58 continues. Let's get a running start from the beginning of verse one: **"Cry loudly, do not hold back; raise your voice like a trumpet, and declare to My people their transgression."** *Transgression.* Sin. Uh-oh.

DON'T BE AFRAID

When you heard the word *sin*, you probably thought you were gonna get blasted, right? "Oh, you wicked, awful sinner!" Wrong! That is neither the content nor the tone of what God inspired Isaiah to say. It's more like the prophet is pleading, "Listen, precious one. More than you could even comprehend, it's your sin that keeps you from the incredible grace and greatness of God. Sin distances your heart from the Lord's abundant provision for you. Please don't deny or defend. I beg you to open your heart and begin to honestly address this issue."

Far from condemnation, Isaiah invites us into joyful transformation. Perhaps you've shown that kind of tough love to someone whose sinful habits are destroying him and those he loves. Picture Isaiah coming to you and saying, "That sin in your life? It's keeping you from wealth you can't imagine. But if you face it and forsake it, God will put stuff in its place that's gonna blow you away!"

"Yeah, yeah. 'Blow me away . . . blah blah blah.' I've heard all this before. God does it for others, I'm sure, but not for me." Do you feel like that? Does it seem as if others always experience God in ways that seem to pass you by? Do you observe others being gripped and wonder why it's not happening to you?

You may feel like God is playing some cosmic game of "hide and seek." You look for Him in your Bible and at church and through service, but at times you're tempted to say, "Come out, come out, wherever You are." If this describes your experience, you need to know that this longing you have is a real thing—*it really is going on.* What I mean is you are seeking, and in a way God *is* hiding, and I want to tell you why.

WHEN GOD IGNORES OUR WORSHIP

The answer is right here in Isaiah 58:1–3:

"And declare to My people their transgression . . . Yet they seek Me day by day and delight to know My ways, as a nation that has done righteousness and has not forsaken the ordinance of their God. They ask Me for just decisions, they delight in the nearness of God. 'Why have we fasted and You do not see? Why have we humbled ourselves and You do not notice?'"

Verse 3 describes a common complaint among God's people: "We've humbled ourselves, and You don't notice." One of the things that troubles me when I read Christian books is that people treat God like some subject in an advice column. Attempting to answer questions about God with "it seems to me" is a complete waste of time. What you and I need is not someone's considered opinion about God. We need to hear from God Himself. That's what we are doing right now. Rather than listening to a lot of blah blah blah about why God seems so far away, we are letting God answer the question Himself. "Lord, why does it seem sometimes that I do the things I am supposed to in order to connect with You, and You completely ignore me?"

A man in our church recently said to me, "I come every week. I sit in the right seat. I hold the right book in my hands. I sing the right words to the right songs, but I am just going through the motions! God is not showing up in my life." Ever feel like that? In a moment I am going to show you from Scripture why that happens. But let me start by saying, *it does happen!*

I refuse to deny a reality we both know is happening. Many pastors and Christian authors are afraid to let God be God. They think they're cutting God a break by denying that He is doing something that they can't explain. Living in this kind of denial short-circuits your faith.

Fact is, if it seems like God is keeping His distance and sort of ignoring your attempts to draw near to Him, He might be. *Ouch!* Sorry —but the pain of surgery is the only way to find healing. Now let's consider why God might be holding you at arm's length even as you're doing the things that constitute seeking Him.

AND THE ANSWER IS . . .

So let's get back to the answers found right here in the text—beginning with the word *behold* in verse 3, which means "listen up." As in, listen up to a few reasons why God sometimes ignores our worship.

Reason #1: Our worship is selfish.

"Behold, on the day of your fast you find your desire, and drive hard all your workers." (v. 3)

That phrase *find your desires* means that you already have pretty much everything you want. When we come to church intent on worshiping God, often we're fed up, we're rested up, we're sexed up, we're leisured up—basically satisfied with everything our hearts desire. Then we rush into church almost as an afterthought and say by our actions, "Oh yeah, God, I want You too." And He is like, "Sorry, it doesn't work that way." You cannot have everything your heart desires *and* God!

If you doubt that, try a little experiment. Right now you are reading a book on how to connect with the Lord in a more intimate and impactful way. We are using the term *gripped* to describe that experience. You must really want it, because you've stayed with it. Try this experiment: Set the book down for a while and go eat a big meal. In fact, eat it in front of the TV while you watch your favorite video. When you're done stuffing yourself, lie down on the couch as the movie continues. If possible, choose a film that shows total disrespect for the things of God. When you are done, come back to this book and see how much energy you have to read it. The answer will be little or none. Creeping up in the back of your mind as you try to read should be a sense of futility or even hypocrisy.

Deep down, we know that we cannot have God *and* the constant satisfaction of every earthly whim. As obvious as that seems, most Christians believe that only sin hinders their relationship with God. That's why Isaiah focuses on fasting. Fasting, as prescribed in Scripture, elevates our hunger and passion for God.

Without a doubt, spending our energy to satisfy our flesh inevitably creates apathy toward God. I believe that's why there is so much spiritual shallowness in the Western world. We think that our material blessings are a sign of God's favor upon us. Wrong! They're probably more a judgment than a blessing. Maybe it's time we honestly recognized financial prosperity for what it often is: not so much a blessing from God but the result of having systematically neglected the priority of our relationship with Him.

This phrase "you find your desire" is God's way of saying you can't have your cake and eat it too! "The reason I don't show up in your worship is because you have no room left to sincerely hunger for Me." Remember Jesus' words: **"Blessed are those who hunger and thirst for righteousness, for they shall be satisfied"** (Matthew 5:6). It seems you can only be filled when you have an empty place to hold what God longs to give you. Bottom line: God won't be hurried and He's not your hobby.

God will be your *hunger* or nowhere to be found!

Secondly, God doesn't show up in your worship because **"you drive hard all your workers"** (v. 3b), another expression of selfishness. Here Isaiah is saying that even though you set aside time to attend a worship service, your investment machine keeps on going. You may be at church, but your cell phone and pager are still on, and your little system of generating income is still in gear, even if it's just in your thoughts. You would never *think* of shutting them down to give your full and focused attention to God and to God alone.

Or maybe when you are on the job you are not that nice to the people you work with. If you or your spouse have employees, are they rewarded for loyalty and hard work, or do you squeeze them for every nickel you can make? Do you fight to see that company profits are equitably distributed, or do you support a system that gets more to those who need it least? God cares very deeply about these matters of justice. We can't ignore this subject and then act surprised if God ignores our worship. He will only grip our hearts with the joy of His presence when we seek Him on His terms. **"A God of truth and without iniquity, just and right is he"** (Deuteronomy 32:4 KJV).

The bottom line is: We cannot compartmentalize work and worship, expecting the latter to be powerful with God when the former is punishing others. Next time you feel like a wallflower at a worship service, watching others' enthusiasm and wondering why you can't seem to enter in, ask yourself honestly, "Am I a bit selfish? Have I been consumed with what will meet my needs, even to the expense of others? Do I worship God in order to get some supernatural zing? Is He just another item on my 'feel good' list? If yes, I must not be surprised if God shakes His head and says, 'Go ahead; do your thing. But don't expect Me to be part of it.'"

God is either 24/7/365 in the midst of all we are and do—or He won't show up at all.

Reason #2: We are strife-filled.

Christians can sometimes be directionally challenged. Some are consumed with the vertical and think they can avoid or ignore the horizontal. Maybe you have some horizontal stuff (with people) that you need to deal with before you can get the vertical thing right with God. Notice verse 4 says, **"Behold, you fast** [you seek God in a worshipful way] **for contention and strife and to strike with a wicked fist."** In other words, you fuss and fume and fight with people all week, and then you come to worship. Instead of leaving church determined to get right with people and be an instrument of reconciliation in this world, you walk out and, before you get one hundred yards, pound the steering wheel over a traffic jam in the parking lot. Or you crab at the kids all the way home.

In the middle of all of that, you try to fold in some genuine, personal relationship with God. God is saying, "You're kidding, right? You want *Me* to connect with you when you're like this?" God doesn't meet with us when our lives are filled with strife.

From the very beginning, my wife and I have had a ministry dream that is kind of rare these days. While we were in seminary we prayed, "Lord, we will go wherever You want us to go, but we want to stay there." Our vision was for a lifetime of ministry in one place with the same group of people.

Growing up I had observed that pastors often moved on when the congregation became aware of their shortcomings or when the pastor grew weary of where certain church leaders needed to grow. We envisioned a church where pastor and people loved and accepted one another, all the while praying and rejoicing in God's ongoing work of transformation.

Seventeen years into it, I can tell you for a fact that our vision is a lot easier to put on paper than to put into practice. Many times I have wanted to pack up all the lessons I have learned and go somewhere safe to begin again. It's not so much the shortcomings of others that make it tough to persevere—it's my own failures and areas of weakness. Without a doubt, there are those who have been injured by our commitment to truth telling in all relationships. Most often because they refused to hear the truth, but sadly, sometimes, especially in the early days, because of the manner in which I told it. Of course, the result is relational strife and disappointment among followers of Jesus. What has surprised me most of all in this is how easily Christians can "move on," without seeking repeatedly to bring these matters to a place of forgiveness and reconciliation.

> **Y**ou can't have the vertical thing right with Him if you haven't at least done your part to make the horizontal relationships right.

Amazingly, a lot of Christians still think they can be right with God, i.e., vertically, when they have not done the horizontal work of seeking to be right with others. God has taught me this the hard way.

Paul tells us, **"If possible, so far as it depends on you, be at peace with all men"** (Romans 12:18). Jesus says in Matthew 5:23 that if you come to worship God, and while you're at the altar you remember a problem you have with somebody, you should leave your sacrifice and go make the relationship right. Just get up and walk out, get on the phone, or write the letter or, get in your car and get over to that house. Humble yourself before that person and say, "I'm so sorry for what's happened. Please forgive me."

I know that this sometimes involves matters that are very complex. Believe me, *I know*. When two followers of Christ see a difficult situation differently, reconciliation becomes extremely challenging. We are not to compromise the truth or make "peace at all cost." What we are commanded to do is to humble ourselves, admitting the wrong *we have* done, and then leave the rest with the Lord. **"If possible, so far as it depends on you, be at peace with all men"** (Romans 12:18).

A man I'll call Bill comes to our church every Sunday morning and sits in the front center section with his wife—that is, his second wife. Years ago, Bill was a leader in a church, but he chose to walk away from the Lord. Bill allowed himself to fall in love with a woman who was not his wife and eventually left his wife to marry her. Of course, he lost his position as a leader and was put under church discipline for his sin.

At that point, Bill showed up on our doorstep with this other woman. Before we were even aware that Bill was attending, the pastor of his former church called me to relay the story of his rebellion. Wanting to be supportive of their leadership, we asked Bill for a meeting and challenged him to turn back to Christ and return to his wife. Amazingly, he told us, "Even though what I am doing is wrong, I will not repent. I am going to marry this woman and then tell God I am sorry and seek His forgiveness." Of course, we warned him of the danger of trying to play games with God, but Bill went out and did exactly what he wanted.

Four years later, his new wife has professed faith in Christ and is growing in her faith, but Bill sits there every Sunday morning stunned and silent, wondering why God is holding him at arm's length. The man has never made things right with his first wife or children (I pray he will one day), yet he maintains the charade of worshiping God.

Of course, God isn't into games. You don't have to guess what pleases or displeases Him. You may not have done anything as extreme as Bill, but the principle remains the same. When we have not made every effort we can to be right with others, God ignores our worship.

Reason #3: We are surface-y.

We may look really sincere. We may make all the right moves, but God ignores our worship when we're focused on externals. You can see it in verse 5. Notice God says, "Is it a fast like this which I choose? . . . Is it for bowing one's head like a reed?" In other words, did God ask that you bow low to the ground like some cattails on a windy day? God says, "Is that what I'm into?"

"And for spreading out sackcloth and ashes as a bed?" (v. 5). Sackcloth was a coarse cloth made of goats' hair. Think of burlap. In the Old Testament, people who wanted to show that they were really serious with God wore this abrasive, rough clothing against their skin as a symbolic expression of their heartfelt brokenness. Then to make themselves even more uncomfortable, they would dump ashes on their head. By radically rejecting all matters related to external appearance, they pictured a consuming concern for their hearts. They were acknowledging how completely disinterested God is in externals and how entirely focused He is with our heart—our thoughts, our attitudes, and our motivations.

As with most symbolic expressions of worship, over time the people became guilty of offering God the symbol and not the reality. They came to worship decked out in burlap and soot, but they failed to let the reality of their sinfulness penetrate their own heart. God was saying, "Do you think that's where I'm at? I couldn't care less about what you're wearing or what you dump on your head. Don't give Me the symbol; give Me the reality!"

Let's talk about some contemporary equivalents. What if you raise your hands to God, a symbol of sincerity and purity—not out of a heightened sense of God's presence in your worship but just because the music is climaxing or because the person beside you does? What if you kneel to pray but on the inside you refuse to yield to what He has been pursuing and convicting you about? How about sitting in church with your Bible open but your heart closed? Or rushing to Bible study with a proud and unreachable spirit? Worst of all, how do you think God feels when we casually take the Communion bread and cup? Imbibing the symbols of our most precious realities even as our minds wander to trivia and fail to seriously scour the hearts Christ died to cleanse?

Those are the times when God ignores our worship. When we come thinking, "What's in this for me?" When we come without doing the horizontal forgiveness. When we look the part and do the externals, but our hearts are far from God. So many people feel frustrated that their worship is formulaic and futile. Sadly, when we sing in this frame of mind, God puts His fingers in His ears.

But not always.

WHEN GOD *IGNITES* OUR WORSHIP

> God ignites our worship when we experience the freedom of Christ.

Then there are the times when God shows up in our lives in wonderful, glorious ways, and it rocks our world. How long since you experienced His presence this way? When His greatness gripped your heart and broke you down, but, wow, it built you up too?

You say, "That's what I want!" And I say, "Me too!" Not wanting this to be a mystery, God laid out the details to Isaiah about when He will show up to powerfully ignite our worship with His awesome presence.

Do you long to feel His grip more consistently and fully? Read on.

In Isaiah 58:6, God describes His kind of worship. He says, **"Is this not the fast which I choose, to loosen the bonds of wickedness, to undo the bands of the yoke, and to let the oppressed go free, and break every yoke?"** That phrase **"bonds of wickedness"** is a picture of a person who is chained to sin.

Do you know what it's like to be chained to sin? I do. Do you know what it's like to be chained to anger, chained to deceit, chained to lust, chained to greed? Try as you might to get free and live the way God wants you to live, somehow it's just not happening. Like some beast who stepped on a trap in the forest, you feel unable to get free. But in verse 6, Isaiah looks ahead to the ministry of Christ and pictures freedom that's for everyone.

> God ignites our worship when we express the compassion of Christ.

Christ has come **"to undo the bands of the yoke."** A yoke is that huge wooden beam that binds two oxen together when they plow, or two horses when they pull. Wherever they go, they go together. Sometimes we're like that with sin. It seems as if no matter how hard we pull and fuss and even run to escape, we cannot get away from certain sins in our life. As in, *wherever I go, it goes with me!*

What's that thing in your life right now? The good news of the gospel can break that yoke and give that sin the shove once and for all.

When we come together to worship God, we're coming together to celebrate the freedom Christ died and rose again to provide. When we are experiencing that in our lives, we can say, "I may not be perfect or have it together totally, but by God's grace, I've had some real victory this week. I used to do *X*, but I don't do that anymore; now I do *Y*." The bondage of sin has been broken in my life. The yoke has been thrown off. I'm experiencing true freedom, and it comes from my relationship with Christ.

God sees people sincerely worshiping Him and says, "When you get a group of people together who are experiencing the freedom that only I can bring, I'll be there in the middle of that party, for sure!" The apostle Paul and Jesus echo Isaiah's cry for freedom:

> *It was for freedom that Christ set us free; therefore keep standing firm and do not be subject again to a yoke of slavery.*
> (Galatians 5:1)

> *"So if the Son makes you free, you will be free indeed."* (John 8:36)

Now the issue moves from character on the inside to behavior on the outside. From the root to the fruit. In other words, if you're experiencing freedom on the inside, it's going to show up in your actions.

Let's continue Isaiah 58 with verse 7. **"Is it not to divide your bread with the hungry and bring the homeless poor into the house; when you see the naked, to cover him; and not to hide yourself from your own flesh?"**

Isaiah lists several compassions which confirm the reality of Christ in our lives—the first of which is compassion for the hungry.

Compassion for the Hungry

Read any book in the Bible carefully and you can't avoid God's heart for the hungry. Sadly, though, we fall way short of implementing His orders. In regard to serving those with hunger needs we tend to say, "I have ten loaves; you can have one. I have a hundred loaves; you can have some." To help the hungry doesn't mean saying, "I have plenty; here's a bit from my overflow." True biblical compassion gives to meet needs until it actually involves personal sacrifice. "I have *just enough,* but you can have some of it. I'll have a little less than I absolutely ideally need so that you can have some too." You say, "James, I don't know anything about that."

Change Starts with Honesty

I'll be honest. I don't know a lot about that kind of compassion either. But I am very convinced that when we give with that kind of sacrifice, we reflect God's heart. We can't close our hearts to the needs of the world and expect God to grip us and our families in our worship.

A Heart for the Helpless

God says, "This is the fast that I've chosen . . . To bring the homeless poor into the house." Isaiah isn't standing there with a bucket asking for your spare change. He's not telling you to send a check so that someone in Cleveland or Cambodia can have a roof over their heads (though that's a good thing to do). It's not even about picking up a homeless person in your car and taking him to the rescue mission. It's more like allowing someone with massive needs to come and stay with you and sticking with them until his or her life is back on track. That's compassion. That's when God says, "I'm showing up in their lives powerfully and often."

The Lord taught Kathy and me about this kind of sacrifice early in our marriage. The first person to live with us was a needy college student named Pam. She had no one to turn to in a rather large city and had known Kathy a little bit during their high school days. She was estranged from her family and seemed to be open to learning about the Lord. For many months after long days of ministry, Kathy and I shared our little home and our "newlywed" evenings with Pam. We brought her to church with us and pressed her consistently about the claims of Christ.

That was many years ago now, and I am not even sure where Pam is today, but I do know this: She was the first in a steady stream of people who have enriched our lives, impacted our children, and had their lives affected by living in our home. Rebellious teens, couples on the verge of divorce, lonely people looking for a place to be known and loved have filled our lives with God's kind of joy. Best of all, I believe that the Lord's grace in our lives, our abiding sense of His presence, and an almost continuous outpouring of abundance and blessing are directly related to these decisions of compassion—ironclad proof that **"losing your life"** for the sake of others is a sure way to find it (Matthew 16:25).

Remember, God cares about people who no one else cares about— the hungry. The homeless. The helpless. **"When you see the naked, to cover him"** (v. 7). That *nakedness* is a picture of helplessness. Rather than seeing a naked person and saying, "Tsk-tsk! How immodest!" God calls us to recognize the need and do all we can to meet it. It always amazes me that parents who want so much for their kids to embrace the gospel are so slow to see that living it out in practical, compassionate ways before their eyes is the strongest message of all. **"Let your light shine before men in such a way that they may see your good works, and glorify your Father who is in heaven"** (Matthew 5:16).

Compassion on the Home Front

Isaiah continues to define compassion: **"Not to hide yourself from your own flesh."** "Own flesh" is a reference to your family. Not

131

the people in your church or on your street, but the people who sleep under your roof at night. At my graduation ceremony from Trinity Divinity School, Chuck Swindoll shared a message entitled "Five Things They Never Taught Me in Seminary." I've never forgotten one of his points. He said, "It's hardest at home." As hard as it is to pick up a homeless person or feed a hungry person, the hardest place to live out the truth of the gospel is at home.

How many men sit in church week after week next to their emotionally starved wives? How many wives wonder why God won't answer their prayers yet are blind to the ways they continuously reject the protective covering God has provided in their own husbands? I know many heartbroken parents long for a genuine word of appreciation from their children (especially their adult children).

God won't meet you at church on Sunday if His ways have been banned from your home throughout the week.

"But you don't know how hard my situation is," you say. After years of intense ministry, I can tell you that circumstances are not as different as you may think they are. God's grace and God's strength are available for whatever your family needs. If we're not sincerely trying to apply these truths, then it's not right for us to wonder why God doesn't manifest Himself more obviously in our own individual or corporate worship.

OK, enough of why God doesn't show up in our worship. What does it look like when He does? Great question!

WORSHIP LOOKS LIKE THIS

Beginning in verse 8, God is telling us, "When you choose the fast that I choose, when you worship Me the way that I want to be worshiped, when you're experiencing the freedom of Christ and ministering the compassion of Christ, then when we get together—get set!"

Isaiah 58 describes five different ways we know God is igniting our worship with Himself. Look at verses 8–9:

"Then your light will break out like the dawn, and your recovery will speedily spring forth; and your righteousness will go before you; the glory of the LORD will be your rear guard.

Then you will call, and the LORD will answer; You will cry, and He will say, 'Here I am.'"

#1: Light
"Then your light will break out like the dawn." (v. 8)

Many verses in the Bible describe a dynamic, personal relationship with God as "light" and a believer who lives in fellowship with God as "walking in God's light." I can't explain God's light to you. I just know the Bible refers to it over and over and over again. When Moses came down from Mount Sinai, his face glowed (Exodus 34:29). When Jesus was transfigured before the disciples, His face shone like the sun (Matthew 17:2). How appropriate then that Christ promises in Matthew 13:43 that **"the righteous will shine forth as the sun in the kingdom of their Father."**

GET A GRIP ON GOD'S GREATNESS
The Glory of God
**"I have created [you] for My glory . . .
I have formed [you]."** (Isaiah 43:7)

*G*od made us so that we could reflect His glory back to Him. *Glory* is to God as wet is to water, as heat is to fire, as light is to bulb. Glory is what emanates from God. Although we can't see God (1 John 4:12), we can see His glory in creation and in His people when they model His holiness. Glory is the evidence that God is present.

God's purpose in your life is to bring glory to or display Himself. In fact, He wants to do it even in the most mundane things that you do. **"Whether . . . you eat or drink or whatever you do, do all to the glory of God"** says 1 Corinthians 10:31. In commanding us to glorify Him, God invites us to leave His fingerprints on everything we touch.

Notice Isaiah said that your light will "break out." Have you ever been up before dawn, perhaps on a night when some crisis robbed you of sleep? For hours the world is shrouded in darkness, and then suddenly the black horizon turns navy, then purple, then lavender, then—pow!—the sun breaks through! Isaiah says that when God shows up in your life, you will shine like *that*. Light spills over from your life into a dark world. God's glory, the evidence of His presence, shines in us as we engage in genuine worship. Jesus said, **"You are the light of the world"** (Matthew 5:14).

#2: Recovery
"And your recovery will speedily spring forth." (v. 8)

The word *recovery* means wholeness, or health. God's presence in response to our sincere worship brings recovery. Do you need physical healing? Do you have some scars from the past that your wounded heart won't let recover? You ask, "When will God heal these things?" The promise here is that **"your recovery will speedily spring forth."** We see many shysters in the church today who guarantee physical healing and set their hopeful audience up for shame and disappointment.

Then there are those who relegate the healing ministry of Christ to a "different dispensation." Hiding their lack of faith behind their theological system, they keep God's people from experiencing the healing God does want to bring. God does heal—not on demand and not in every circumstance, but He does both physically and emotionally heal. Between those two extremes is the historic consensus of the church of Jesus Christ.

If you need healing in mind or in body, I want you to remember that until God's power is revealed in our midst, neither is possible. The recovery that God brings comes only through His manifest presence in response to sincere worship.

#3: Righteousness
"And your righteousness will go before you." (v. 8)

In moments of real honesty, most believers will admit to the pain of battling certain "besetting sins." *Why do I keep doing that? When will I ever get victory over this? Will this always be a struggle for me?*

God says, "When I show up in response to your worship, you have the power to conquer that thing that is keeping you down." Maybe victory over sin has been more absent than present in your life. That can change!

> **When we allow God's righteousness to reign in our lives, we begin to see change and growth and transformation in our lives.**

As 2 Corinthians 2:14 says, **"But thanks be to God, who always leads us in triumph in Christ, and manifests through us the sweet aroma of the knowledge of Him in every place."** This verse pictures a Roman victory parade. God, the conquering warrior, has defeated our enemies and leads those of us who have been "taken captive by Christ" to His home. At the head of this victory parade, incense is burned—and its strong fragrance, here compared to the knowledge of Christ, went everywhere.

Now, these are all things that God wants to do *for you.* You can't get victory in your own strength. You can't become a different person out of sheer willpower because you say, "I'm not doing that anymore!" Romans 8:8 says that **"those who are in the flesh cannot please God."** Exodus 14:14 says that **"the Lord will fight for you."** God's presence in response to sincere worship means true victory. Woohoo!

#4: Protection
"The glory of the LORD will be your rear guard." (v. 8)

So there you are—experiencing the presence of God in your life. You're walking in the light. Experiencing recovery. Growing in His righteousness. You are capturing serious ground from the enemy and moving forward for God.

But just then, when you least expect it, something happens, and you feel like you've been stabbed in the back.

God says here in verse 8, **"The glory of the LORD will be your rear guard."** *Rear guard* is a military term. When God led the children of Israel out of Egypt, He led them with a pillar of fire. But when they got through the Red Sea, the pillar went around behind them and protected them so that their enemies would not recapture their newly taken ground (Exodus 14:19).

God says, "I want our victories to last forever! No more winning the battle but losing the war. No more temporary transformation that morphs back into the old you." God's presence in response to sincere worship protects us from going retro. No more short-lived successes, but permanent victory!

#5: Full provision
"Then you will call, and the LORD will answer; you will cry, and He will say, 'Here I am.'"(v. 9)

"Here I am!" God says. "What took you so long to turn to Me?" Jesus said "How many times I was willing, but *you* were not willing" (see Luke 13:34).

But now the game is over. No more hide-and-seek with God. No more wandering and wondering when God will again make His presence known. Read verse 9 again. Isn't that the kind of walk with God every believer longs for? I call and He answers quickly with the comforting affirmation, **"Here I am."** Wow, more of that, please!

When I was a kid, I had a strong tendency to focus on the benefits and forget the path I had to follow to get there. I was big on outcome and short on process. All about the sweet desserts but not much for the vegetables and meat you had to swallow to get there. Can you relate? That dynamic is often present in our relationship with God. I talk to so many Christians who are aggravated that God has not done some of the things He promised in their life, yet *they* have not met God's conditions. They still insist on doing the Christian life their own way, refusing to come to God on the terms that He has laid down so clearly and repeatedly. If only they would seek God where He told them He could be found. God promises to do great things in our lives, but He reminds us of the ground rules.

"If you remove the yoke from your midst, the pointing of the finger and speaking wickedness, and if you give yourself to the hungry and satisfy the desire of the afflicted, then . . ." (vv. 9–10)

The first rule is to take an honest look at yourself.

The yoke Isaiah is talking about here is the yoke of sin. We must eliminate all known sin both in attitude and action. We must repent of the ways we have failed the Lord and seek His grace to begin again. The pointing finger pictures our attitudes toward others. You know what I mean—the feelings of superiority we quietly nurture in our garden of pride. The critical comments, thought or spoken, that tear others down and dispel the presence of God who loves them just as much as He loves us.

The second rule is be willing to meet the needs of those around you as often as you can. God's presence quickly stalls in a stingy heart. But if we are generous and quick to share what we have with those who have not, then . . . then and only then can we expect the unparalleled delight of reveling in the manifest presence and power of God.

TELL ME AGAIN ABOUT GOD'S PRESENCE . . .

Never forget that *all* the human heart longs for is experienced in the manifest presence of God. It was Augustine who said that our hearts are restless until they find rest in Him. Recounting the numberless blessings of the life lived in God, John Wesley said, "Best of all, God is with us." Isaiah describes it this way: **"Then your light will rise in darkness and your gloom will become like midday"** (v. 10). All that we are will rise into the light of who God is and dispel the darkness that hangs over our world and too often over our own hearts.

Here's the equation:

Clean on the inside + compassion on the outside = God in the midst.

Isaiah's full promise is this:

"Then your light will rise in darkness and your gloom will be-come like midday. And the LORD will continually guide you, and satisfy your desire in scorched places, and give strength to your bones; and you will be like a watered garden, and like a spring of water whose waters do not fail." (vv. 10–11)

If the truth were known, a lot of Christians are gloomy, discouraged, and depressed, looking for all kinds of medicated or worldly answers, when God says, "I would meet that need in your life. I would turn your gloom to bright sunshine."

Some of you have been living in a scorched place. Your life has felt like ground zero. You wonder, *Will anything ever grow in my life again?* We're right on the bull's-eye here of how that can happen. God will **"give strength to your bones; and you will be like a watered garden."** If you've ever wondered not when but if your heart to worship will ever return, I can tell you the answer is "yes, it can" because— you guessed it . . .

It Happened to Me

MIRACLE IN ELGIN

My wife and I began Harvest Bible Chapel in the late 1980s with a committed group of pioneers and a vision to see God powerfully at work. Of course, we have had our setbacks and challenges (I often joke, "I gave up my hair for this church"), but for the most part, we have been witness to a sustained display of God's greatness.

By the time Harvest Bible Chapel was thirteen years old, our weekly services were maxed out—we couldn't add any more services; we couldn't add any more parking. It was obvious that we needed to find new property, large enough and close enough on which to relocate. After two agonizing years, we discovered a piece of land perfectly suited for our needs. Problem: The property was owned by the Catholic Church, and they don't sell much—especially not to an evangelical church. Nevertheless, our church's history is one of multiplied miraculous answers to prayer, and so we set about to test the promises of God.

I filled my heart with faith based on Mark 11:24, **"All things for which you pray and ask, believe that you have received them and they will be granted you,"** and I repeatedly went out on the property to walk and pray. Our elders gathered on the vacant land holding hands in a circle, calling out to God by faith and asking Him to give us this land.

Behind the scenes it really appeared as if He would. Doors that were previously slammed shut began to open. Key people within the ranks of the Catholic hierarchy began to soften to the idea of selling us the land, even to the point of contacting us and inviting an offer. I continued to pray as the private negotiations accelerated, telling our church on several occasions that a miracle was imminent that would "blow their minds." So focused I became on "claiming this mountain" that I hardly thought of anything else.

I begged God to do this work and put myself in a very dangerous position spiritually. Psalm 106:15 says God **"gave them their request, but sent leanness into their soul"** (NKJV).

God doesn't want us to long for His works more than we long for Him. God is not a heavenly genie waiting reluctantly till we rub the lamp the right way. We must be very careful of begging God to do some specific work in a way that quenches our thirst for Him and His greatness alone.

Praying and pleading for a specific something as I had been made me very vulnerable. So when the news came that we would not be getting the property, I was devastated. More than ever before, I faced a crisis in my own faith, finding it so hard to understand why God would have refused the only possibility for our future that I could see. I struggled so much that I changed my preaching plan and started a new series, "God @ Work, Even When I'm Not Seeing It."

In this study, as much for my own benefit as it was for our church's, I searched God's Word for hope that He works even when we can't see it. I studied Jacob, who said, **"Surely the LORD is in this place, and I did not know it"** (Genesis 28:16). I studied the plan of God that silently unfolded in the book of Ruth. I preached on Esther, an amazing Old Testament book that tells of God's great work without even mentioning His name. This was the final six weeks of 2002 and then into January of 2003. Where are You, God? What are You doing? I believe You're working, but I am sure not seeing it.

That painful prayer was more accurate than I could have imagined.

Late in January, we were made aware of a corporate building on eighty-five acres of land twenty miles away from our church location. We hadn't considered it before because it was outside our search area. We needed to stay close to our current location, because we would need to sell it in order to get into a new property, or so it seemed to our finite minds.

This new property was owned by the Green family from Oklahoma City; you might know them as the owner of the store chain Hobby Lobby. The property included a 285,000-square-feet building on a major four-lane road west of Elgin, Illinois, with a 900-car parking garage. It was purchased and built in 1993 at a cost of $53 million.

But get this (this is amazing)—this property was available as a gift from the Greens to a ministry of their choice, with the specification that the property could not be resold, that the recipient must demonstrate a similarity of conviction and a readiness to bear the financial cost of developing the site into a meaningful center of gospel ministry.

Understandably, I was very excited, because the nature of this amazing gift would allow us to expand our ministry as a multi-campus church, remaining at our current site. The opportunity seemed perfect beyond words, but I determined in my heart I would never again get attached to a particular property as God's will for our church. I wanted to want God Himself and all His works, not a particular possibility that appeared the way He should do it.

We flew to Oklahoma City, met this wonderful family, and made our vision for the property known. I will never forget their words at our departure. "Well, everyone has told us what they believe God wants to do; now we're waiting for God to vote, and when He does, we'll let you know." Before, that would have seemed so far out of my control, but now it was perfect. I was resting by faith, and by God's grace ready for what He would do next.

We were told by the Green family that we were in the final running for the property with Jerry Falwell of Liberty University. I had never met Dr. Falwell, but like most Americans, I was familiar with his ministry. To me, he seemed larger than life. Imagine then my shock when in February 2003, he rang my cell phone. (I still don't know how he got the number.) He introduced himself and said, "I understand you're interested in the Hobby Lobby property." "Yes," I answered with a shaky voice, not knowing what *was coming next. "Well," he said, "we are flying down to Oklahoma City tomorrow, and they are going to give the property to us." Gulp.*

At that moment, I was glad that I had been praying with an open heart, because the first words out of my mouth were a lot different than I could have prayed six months earlier. "Well, that's good news for us, Dr. Falwell. We have been praying for God's will to be done, and if that means the property is for you, then we can get on to whatever He has in store for us."

If you know me, that was a real miracle of a response. But our conversation continued. He asked me all about our church and what we were doing, and over the course of the conversation, I sensed a subtle change in his tone. Suddenly he confessed, "You know, James, I am sixty-nine years old, and really have all I can handle right here in Lynchburg. I think I will fly down to Oklahoma City, but I'm going to tell them that they ought to give the property to you." And that is exactly what he did.

Between Dr. Falwell's withdrawal and the Green family's own sense of the Lord's leading, within a few days we received the news that the property was ours! Amazing, awesome provision of God. A 53-million-dollar facility for our church for one dollar. God is able to do "exceedingly, abundantly above all that we ask or think" (Ephesians 3:20 NKJV). We can honestly testify to Psalm 118:23, "This is the LORD's doing; it is marvelous in our eyes."

My oldest son kind of tweaked me when he heard the exciting news. "Wow, I guess you really want that Catholic property now, huh, Dad?" Ouch. What a not-so-gentle reminder to remain confident God is working even when we can't see it. Hopefully you can avoid the painful valley of doubt that came to me as a result of wanting a specific work of God rather than His plan, in His timing, in His way.

Here's the lesson: God must be God, and He will be. Our choices are worshipful submission or stubborn rebellion. Either we get to participate in the ultimate wisdom of what God is doing by choosing to worship at all times now, or we miss the joy of partnership in His purposes by standing on the side with folded arms, expecting God to explain Himself. How strongly I commend to you that first choice no matter how tough it may be in this moment. Choose to worship; choose words of praise and gratitude no matter how haltingly they come at first. Worship like that will find for you the fountain of joy reserved for those who want more than a simple surface faith. I can tell you that for sure, not just because I've seen it in others but because
it happened to me.

WHAT ABOUT YOU?

Has Isaiah 58 given you a renewed vision of what your life can be like with God in the center and on the throne? He may not be there right now, but He's waiting. In order for your worship of God to grip you with His greatness, you may have some hard work ahead of you. Take what you've learned from our study and bring it to God in humble submission. The wonder of getting lost in His worship and praise waits for you up ahead. Don't miss another day. **"Great is the LORD, and highly to be praised"** (Psalm 145:3). Let that greatness grip you as never before.

LET'S PRAY

Oh worthy God,

I open my heart to Thee and confess to You the places in my life that I have kept separate from my worship of You.

I acknowledge that my attitude toward _____ has been wrong, and I ask Your forgiveness.

I repent of my lack of compassion toward those in need (of my love, of my service, of my time, of my financial gifts). I think especially of _____. Please help me as I strive to replace my stinginess with generosity.

I confess that I have only thought of myself, especially in my relationship with _____. Help me to be like Your Son, who though He is God became a servant. Give me opportunities to serve _____ and then the humility and courage to do it.

I confess to You my surface-y approach to worship. I long to worship You in spirit and truth, with all my heart, no matter what happens in my life. Keep me from being satisfied with anything less.

I understand that You may be ignoring my worship right now because I have been trying to live the Christian life on my own terms. I repent of that right now, Lord, _____ (fill in date, time) and come to You on Your terms.

With faith, I anticipate what You will do in my life in the coming hours, days, and weeks as I bow before You in sincere worship. I believe that even now You are flooding my life with the reality of who You are. Thank You, Father. May Your greatness be lifted up before and exalted in and through me.

—*Amen.*

MAKE IT PERSONAL

1. In this chapter we talked about three reasons why God would ignore our worship:

   > Reason #1: Our worship is selfish.
   > Reason #2: We are strife-filled.
   > Reason #3: We are surface-y.

   Go before the Lord with an open heart and a blank piece of paper. Ask Him to reveal the areas of change you must make in your life to make your worship acceptable to Him. It may mean a change in your attitude toward someone in your family or at work. It may mean confession of and repentance from a certain sin. It may mean a completely transformed approach to Sunday—or the days in between Sundays. Wait before the Lord with patience and sincerity, and He will show you these things. Get your pen moving on the paper, and you'll be surprised by new insights into your own heart.

   Then, only after your paper is filled, think of one way (or a hundred ways!) that you can specifically model Christ's compassion. We talked about several in this chapter. Make it a deliberate choice to put His heart in action in your life. Tell a friend of your desire to worship God in this way, and ask him or her to keep you accountable to do it.

2. Read these seven Scripture passages that describe various benefits that we have as God's "children of light." Write out a principle for living after each passage that will encourage you to walk with Him today. Share your conclusions with a friend.

   Psalm 89:15 _____

   Psalm 119:105 _____

   Proverbs 4:18 _____

   Proverbs 6:20–23 _____

   Isaiah 2:5 _____

Ephesians 5:7–10 _____

1 John 1:7 _____

3. Meditate on Isaiah 58:8–9. How has God's greatness been manifested in your life in these five categories? How has His greatness changed you in the last twelve hours? In the last week? Month? Watch for these blessings as you embrace a lifestyle of worship:

1. **Light**—*"Then your light will break out like the dawn."*
2. **Recovery**—*"And your recovery will speedily spring forth."*
3. **Righteousness**—*"And your righteousness will go before you."*
4. **Protection**—*"The glory of the LORD will be your rear guard."*
5. **Full provision**—*"Then you will call, and the LORD will answer; you will cry, and He will say, 'Here I am.'"*

Israel Redeemed

But now, thus says the LORD, your Creator, O Jacob,
And He who formed you, O Israel,
"Do not fear, for I have redeemed you;
I have called you by name; you are Mine!
When you pass through the waters, I will be with you;
And through the rivers, they will not overflow you.
When you walk through the fire, you will not be scorched,
Nor will the flame burn you.
For I am the LORD your God,
The Holy One of Israel, your Savior;
I have given Egypt as your ransom,
Cush and Seba in your place.
Since you are precious in My sight,
Since you are honored and I love you,
I will give other men in your place and other peoples in exchange for your life.
Do not fear, for I am with you;
I will bring your offspring from the east,
And gather you from the west.
I will say to the north, 'Give them up!'
And to the south, 'Do not hold them back.'
Bring My sons from afar
And My daughters from the ends of the earth,
Everyone who is called by My name,
And whom I have created for My glory,
Whom I have formed, even whom I have made."

Israel Is God's Witness

Bring out the people who are blind, even though they have eyes,
And the deaf, even though they have ears.
All the nations have gathered together
So that the peoples may be assembled.
Who among them can declare this
And proclaim to us the former things?
Let them present their witnesses that they may be justified,
Or let them hear and say, "It is true."
"You are My witnesses," declares the LORD,
"And My servant whom I have chosen,
So that you may know and believe Me
And understand that I am He.

Before Me there was no God formed,
And there will be none after Me.
I, even I, am the LORD,
And there is no savior besides Me.
It is I who have declared and saved and proclaimed,
And there was no strange god among you;
So you are My witnesses," declares the LORD,
"And I am God.
Even from eternity I am He,
And there is none who can deliver out of My hand;
I act and who can reverse it?"

Babylon to Be Destroyed

Thus says the LORD your Redeemer, the Holy One of Israel,
"For your sake I have sent to Babylon,
And will bring them all down as fugitives,
Even the Chaldeans, into the ships in which they rejoice.
I am the LORD, your Holy One,
The Creator of Israel, your King."
Thus says the LORD,
Who makes a way through the sea
And a path through the mighty waters,
Who brings forth the chariot and the horse,
The army and the mighty man
(They will lie down together and not rise again;
They have been quenched and extinguished like a wick):
"Do not call to mind the former things,
Or ponder things of the past.
Behold, I will do something new,
Now it will spring forth;
Will you not be aware of it?
I will even make a roadway in the wilderness,
Rivers in the desert.
The beasts of the field will glorify Me,
The jackals and the ostriches,
Because I have given waters in the wilderness
And rivers in the desert,
To give drink to My chosen people.
The people whom I formed for Myself
Will declare My praise.

To be gripped by God's greatness is

to understand not only who He is but

who I am because of Him.

Chapter Six

GRIPPED
by My
IDENTITY
in GOD

Isaiah 43:1–21

WHO AM I, really?

Everyone is searching for the answer to that question, but sadly the quest has taken most of us to some pretty ridiculous places—like our résumés, our relationships, our financial portfolios. None of these however, can reveal more than a mere shadow of who we truly are.

So far we've been gripped by God's greatness in the breathtaking view of His holy throne room, from the stunning heights of His sovereignty, and from His awesome creation back on earth. Now we'll look at how His greatness affects the most secret place in our world—our true identity. Only in our Creator can we discover all we are and were made to become.

When you lose yourself in God's greatness, you find the answers that satisfy every itching in your soul. You are known and loved by the Creator of the universe. Does it get any better than that?

But hang on, I'm getting ahead of myself.

WHAT WERE YOU THINKING?
AS HE THINKS IN HIS HEART, SO IS HE. (PROVERBS 23:7 NKJV)

What are you thinking about right now? The Scripture above makes an unusual promise—that your thoughts determine who you will become. For some of us that's a scary thought, but nevertheless it is true. Especially determinative are what's called *identity thoughts*. These are the thoughts not about where I am or what I am doing but about *who I am!* Thoughts like, "Wow, I am such a loser. Won't I ever learn?" or "People only like me for a while; when they really get to know me they always run away."

The problem is bigger than mere negativity. Some have identity thoughts that are way too positive. "Yes, you can count on me. I'll get it done somehow. I always do," or "It doesn't matter what my performance says about me, I'm still the best one for the job." It's our identity thoughts that root attitudes deeply into our hearts.

Attitudes are patterns of thinking formed over a long period of time (see my book *Lord, Change My Attitude* [Moody]), and they are very difficult to change. I often speak with people surprised by their own actions. "How could I have done that?" "I never dreamed I could do something so awful." Often we fail to see that our identity thoughts entrench our attitudes and in the end dictate our very actions. That's why what we think about ourselves is really a big deal. Again, as a person **"thinks within himself, so he is"** (Proverbs 23:7).

PSEUDO SOLUTIONS

Of course, our fellow man is far better at diagnosing the debilitating effects of harmful identity thoughts than he is at finding a solution. Consider these three pseudo solutions.

Pseudo #1: Pump it up, baby!
Recognizing the problems caused by a negative personal identity, some suggest a personal inflation of sorts. They say what you need to do every morning is "psych yourself up!" Look into that mirror and say, "Dude—you're the man!" or "Sister—you have it going on!" Regardless of the wrong you may have done the previous day and

setting aside the matters in which you clearly need to change, you are to look yourself square in the eye and say, "I am still awesome, and today's gonna be the best day of my life."

Of course, the problem with this approach is that you can only lie to yourself for so long. You might say, "I'm a great guy," but you know in your heart you're not. The Bible says the heart is **"deceitful above all things, and desperately sick"** (Jeremiah 17:9 ESV). The constant friction between what you tell yourself and what you know to be true eventually brings you down.

Pseudo #2: Make your mark.

Some of us are far too realistic to *pump it up*—so we try to *build it up* instead. Through our efforts to accomplish, we hope to convince ourselves and others how important we are. In our heads we imagine, "I'll build a company [or a ministry] that will make a phenomenal impact upon others. People will see my work and acknowledge my value!" Most of us have poured far too much energy down that bottomless pit. Fact is, none of us can diagram our lives; nor can we accomplish everything we desire or dream. And if we did, it still wouldn't satisfy our longing for true identity.

Pseudo #3: That Family Feeling

Even those who escape the traps of ego inflation and personal notoriety end up retreating down a dead-end street. Acknowledging the emptiness of personal accomplishment, they pursue instead the road of family pride. Pouring themselves into their marriage and kids, they hope to find at home what they lost on Wall Street. The problem here is that growing a family is not like making cookies. Even if you follow the biblical recipe to the letter, things may come out all wrong. No one can guarantee the obedience of another. If my identity is too tightly attached to my family "success," I am headed for heartbreak in a hurry.

FINDING THE MISSING PIECE

Can you see it? The flashing neon sign that hangs over all of this says, "Duh! *You've left out God.*" In the end there is nothing we can do to generate a message about ourselves that will satisfy the longing in our hearts. Until we can honestly affirm "I am who God says I am and that's all that matters," our lives will be restless indeed. Oh the freedom of saying and meaning, "I'm not who my parents say I am; I am not who my boss or my recent review says I am; I am not who my spouse or even my appearance says I am." *But instead . . .* "I am who *God* says I am."

If you're tired of looking for your true identity in all the wrong places, you're ready for Isaiah 43. Here we find five amazing identity points in God.

#1: GOD IS PERSONAL
"I HAVE CALLED YOU BY NAME." (ISAIAH 43:1)

But now, thus says the LORD, your Creator, O Jacob, and He who formed you, O Israel.

God calls Himself "Lord" here, another name for "covenant keeper." He doesn't draw up contracts with people—He creates a covenant with them. When you fail to live as God directs, He doesn't rant, "You broke your word. We're done!" Why? Because He formed you.

I love that word *formed*. God may have *spoken* the universe into existence, but He *formed* us. Genesis 2:7 uses *formed* to describe the creative process of making man from the dust. Jeremiah 18 uses *formed* to picture how a potter shapes the clay. I loved the days in elementary school when my teacher would get out the pottery wheel. It was so cool to see things formed before your eyes. That is, except when the thing being formed is you—then it's a bit scary, isn't it?

Anticipating that response, the Scripture adds: **"Do not fear, for I have redeemed you."** Before you can even express your heart, He speaks right to it. "I know you're afraid . . . don't be."

In two short phrases God affirms His total, absolute commitment to you. The first is **"for I have redeemed you."** *I've bought you back.* In order for God to have a relationship with you, He had to personally pay for it. And believe me, you're not cheap. Wherever redemption is spoken of in Scripture, there is always a ransom demand, the extreme price that must be paid for the one who was kidnapped. For you, God paid the ransom with the death of His Son, Jesus Christ.

GET A GRIP ON GOD'S GREATNESS
My Rock and My Redeemer

Redeemer" is one of Isaiah's favorite names for God. He used it more than any other biblical writer. God the Redeemer paid the ransom for our souls, doing for us what we could never do. God weaves this ribbon of ransom through the entire Bible. The Old Testament points forward to redemption coming through Jesus Christ (Isaiah 53:6–7). The Gospels introduce us face-to-face to the Lamb of God who takes away the sins of the world (John 1:29). God's Spirit comforts us that our Redeemer lives and intercedes for us (Hebrews 4:14–16). Revelation directs our faith to the future when every tongue will worship, **"Worthy is the Lamb that was slain"** (Revelation 5:12). The ribbon of ransom woven through history ties our hearts to God's heart through the blood of His Son Jesus, our Redeemer.

God's second word of personal commitment is **"I have called you by name"** (v. 1). For the past few years I have struggled with the reality of not knowing all the names of the people in our church. I used to know everyone. But somewhere between hundreds and thousands, I completely lost track. I remember the time I was praying about that. The Lord was like, "James—*I* know their names. It's not about *you* communicating *your* love and care to anyone. It's about *you* taking people to *Me!*" Wow, that was both hard to hear and incredibly freeing.

"You are mine" (v. 1). Kathy and I are blessed with two boys and a little girl. I love my boys, no doubt about it, but there is something unique I have found between a father and a daughter. Often I pull Abby on my lap, hold her tightly, and say, "You're Daddy's girl, right?"

And she'll be like, "Daddy's girl." But do you know what? In the end that's not entirely accurate. *No* one can say "You are mine" with 100 percent integrity and honesty except God. Not your father. Not your mother. Not your friends. Not your spouse. Not your children. But God can say to every single one of His children, "I have called you by name, and you are Mine!"

In the massive sea of humanity, now billions of people, only a few can say God has called them by name. Only a fraction of the world's population have received these incredibly defining words direct from the Creator: **"You are Mine." Jesus tells us, "Many are called, but few are chosen"** (Matthew 22:14). If you are among the few who have been chosen . . . wow!

Identity Point #1: I am chosen.

With all due respect to blood relatives, there is something powerful about being chosen. If you were adopted into a family, you were chosen. Your parents looked around and said, "We want *her.*" Or "We choose *him* to be our son." Did you know that adoption's legal bonds are so strong that an adopted child cannot be disowned?

If you are married, then you also know the wonder of being chosen. Out of all the girls in your high school or college, from all the boys in your city or state, your spouse chose *you* to share his or her name, life, and every experience, good or bad, that will ever come your way.

Some people struggle with this truth. They're like, "How dare God choose one person and not choose another!" If that bugs you, you still have a lot to learn about God. If God wants to make one vessel for honor and one vessel for dishonor (2 Timothy 2:20), that's what it means to be sovereign.

> Even the powerful bonds of human relationships can't compare to the truth that God in His infinite grace chose to set His love upon you!

- **"Because he has loved Me, . . . I will set him securely on high, because he has known My name"** (Psalm 91:14).
- **"Just as He chose us in Him before the foundation of the world"** (Ephesians 1:4).

Somehow, before the world was made, God looked into the future and chose to set His love upon you. (If you still struggle with this, reread chapter 3 on God's sovereignty. It will help you understand why we don't get much input on what God does—and that's a good thing.)

#1 New Identity Applied: Confidence
When you begin to let the truth that God personally chose you settle down into your heart, the result is *confidence*. Isaiah 43:1 says, **"Thus says . . . He who formed you, O Israel, 'Do not fear.'"** The opposite of fear is confidence. When you're gripped by His personal interest in you, you can know with certainty that you are not who your résumé, your performance, your friends or enemies say you are. Instead you accept that you are who *God* says you are. For no good reason of your own, God put you on His most wanted list. Let that reality grip you and shape your identity.

#2: GOD IS PRESENT
"I WILL BE WITH YOU." (ISAIAH 43:2)

A few years ago, a pop song topped the chart touting "God was watching us from a distance." I hate that song! Don't buy into that dreamy, pseudo-theological nonsense. God isn't looking at the Earth like some astronaut from orbit. He doesn't need a telescope to see your need. God is right here with us. *Immanuel*, Isaiah said earlier in 7:14, which means **"God with us"** (Matthew 1:23).

Look at verse 2. **"When you pass through the waters, I will be with you; and through the rivers, they will not overflow you. When you walk through the fire, you will not be scorched, nor will the flame burn you."**

Here's the truth about God. He is with you—especially in hardship. Look at the details:

> *Waters* is a general term. *River* is a specific term.
> *Fire* is a general term. *Flame* is a specific term.

General to specific. God is present not just in the year or in the month or in the day you experience hardship, but He's with you in the hour and in the minute and in the second—in the precise moment of heartache. Psalm 34:18 says that the Lord is near to those who have a broken heart.

God specifically measures your trials. "The heat will be just enough to refine you; I have My hand on the thermostat," He says. "I'm watching. Trust Me!"

It's the same picture in the flood. God says that when you pass through the waters, they will not overflow you. As we face tough times we wonder, *How deep will the water get? How long will I be able to touch bottom?* Then if it gets deeper you think, *How long can I tread water?* But God assures us, "I'm controlling the rising tide. I'm measuring the intensity of this trial." Both pictures shout loud and clear that God is "in the building" and very attentive.

Identity Point #2: I am strong.

Why would a loving God allow this kind of hardship? Answer: to show us how strong we can be in Him. Deep within us is a sinful inclination toward independence. We think we can make it on our own, and we want to prove it. The world mocks and ridicules human weakness and celebrates those who shake their fist and proclaim, "I will survive." Fact is, we are all very weak.

Human strength is an illusion that God is committed to obliterating. He lovingly uses hardship and painful circumstance to teach us how badly we really need Him. Like Paul said in 2 Corinthians 12:10, **"When I am weak, then I am strong."** Only when God shows me how weak I am do I reach for Him like a drowning man. God is committed to making that moment possible for each of us. Then, when you are gripped by God's greatness in your life, you can echo the apostle Paul's victory cry, **"I can do all things through Christ who strengthens me"** (Philippians 4:13 NKJV). Only when we exchange our triple-A battery strength for God's nuclear power do we fully realize the purpose of trials.

Truth about God: He is very specifically present during trials. Corresponding truth about me: I am receiving the precise amount of strength I need, provided I am willing to reach out for it.

#2 New Identity Applied: Perseverance

The other day I was working on the computer with my oldest son, Luke. When he signed on, I asked him, "What's your password?" He said, *"Keep on."* That is a great password. He said, "Oh Dad, that's my password for everything." *Keep on. Keep on. Keep on.* He has no idea how critical those two words are to success in life. The biblical word is "endurance" or "staying power"—the ability to remain under the pressure. Nothing is more essential to success in the Christian life than that. Faith gets you started, but perseverance keeps you going.

Let me say boldy: You are not going to give up! God is present with you, He is giving you the strength that you need, and you are not going under—no way! You are an overcomer in a world of quitters. Let your identity in God grip your heart, shape your thoughts, and dictate the destiny almighty God has ordained for you.

#3: GOD IS LOVING
"YOU ARE PRECIOUS IN MY SIGHT." (ISAIAH 43:4)

Isaiah 43:3–4 will help us understand God's heart. It sounds a bit alien at first, but stay with me:

"For I am the LORD your God, the Holy One of Israel, your Savior; I have given Egypt as your ransom, Cush and Seba in your place."

Where in the world are Cush and Seba? I looked it up; they are provinces in southern Egypt. Isaiah's original audience had slavery on their minds, so God references their ancient history. "Remember when I delivered you out of slavery?" The ransom for their freedom was the lives of the Egyptians. "Remember all that bloodshed? The plagues and then the midnight deaths of the firstborn, etc. Then as you fled, the Egyptian army drowning at the bottom of the Red Sea. Remember? It happened!" Here's the principle: God says, "I will deliver you *even* at the expense of others."

Look at the last three words in verse 3: **"in your place."** The same principle is at the end of verse 4: **"I will give other men in your place and other peoples in exchange for your life."** What a humbling, haunting truth. Both of these phrases refer to the principle of substitutionary atonement. Because of His holiness, God demands that sin be paid for. But because of His love, He allows a substitute.

This principle of substitution is all over the Scripture. Isaiah expands it in chapter 53: "**All we like sheep have gone astray; we have turned, every one, to his own way; and the Lord has laid on Him** [speaking of Christ prophetically] **the iniquity of us all**" (v. 6 NKJV). What the Old Testament pictures and promises the New Testament

> Embrace the message almighty God is singing over you this moment: "You are precious in My sight . . . and I love you!"

provides and proclaims. Second Corinthians 5:21 says, "**He made Him who knew no sin to be sin on our behalf, so that we might become the righteousness of God in Him.**" When I think about all those Egyptians dying at the bottom of the Red Sea rather than the Israelites, it doesn't bother me that much. They were pagans who rejected God; they deserved punishment, and in the end, it was war.

But Jesus dying for you and me is another matter entirely. He was pure and spotless, righteous and holy. He deserved *no* judgment. He took judgment upon Himself as God's Son so that we might be forgiven. Amazing! As we learned in chapter 1, God's holiness demands that sin not be casually dismissed. In order to forgive us, someone had to pay the penalty for our sin.

But why would Jesus choose to do that? The answer is right here in verse 4, "**Since you are precious in My sight, since you are honored and I love you.**" In the original Hebrew language, each of those phrases is in the perfect tense. It describes God's affection for us from eternity past to the present, and forever into the future.

"How could He? I've done some things that I can't even talk about . . ." Wait. You're still not getting it. Let go of the things that have distorted your perspective of who you are. Erase from your mind all distorted perspectives your behavior and pride may have engraved upon your identity.

Identity Point #3: I am valued.

But does God's love make me valuable? Answer: No.

That message is not in the Bible. There is nothing *in us* that makes us valuable. The fact that God *values* us says something about *God*. It says *nothing* about us. God did not set His love upon you because you have something going on that your next-door neighbor doesn't. We are not valuable in ourselves, and believe it or not—that is great news.

Here's the thing: If God loves us because of something He saw in us, then what happens when we change? When we fail, or fall, or fade away? Will God's heart change? Maybe His love goes away. No! The distinction may seem minor, but listen—it's massive. We are not valuable; we are *valued*. Get the difference?

My wife, Kathy, has always enjoyed reading about the Kennedy family. She especially enjoys learning about JFK's wife, who later became Jacqueline Kennedy Onassis. In 1996, Jackie-O's estate was auctioned off, and people went crazy. A worn footstool went for $33,350. A silver tape measure sold for $48,875. (I have *three* of those at home!) The night's highest price was for a walnut tobacco humidor that had belonged to President Kennedy. That stupid cigar box sold for $574,500! Here's the point: That stuff was valued not because of any intrinsic worth, but because of whom it belonged to. It's the same with us. We're the tarnished tobacco box, but we belong to God. My value is not in who I am but in *whose* I am. And unlike some cigar box, God Almighty is eternal, so His love isn't going away.

#3 New Identity Applied: Security

So, if I didn't earn His love; if I didn't pay for it; if I didn't deserve it, then get this—I'm not the one who has to keep it going. I am secure.

Fifty percent of marriages end in divorce. A career job is one that lasts more than five years before the company folds or fires you or finds a new technology to replace you. People change churches like they change their underwear. And the idea "friends for life" seems to have gone the way of ice boxes and typewriters. I can't believe the number of people who have recently said, "Good-bye! We're moving to such-and-such. I got a different job where I'll make an additional 37 cents an hour." "What about the life you've built here?" I ask.

159

With so much rejection swirling in the air, it's no wonder the matter of insecurity is epidemic. Everyone seems to be wondering when the hammer will fall and the pain of broken relationship will be felt yet again.

I love Psalm 11:3, which says, **"If the foundations are destroyed, what can the righteous do?"** Let's build our lives on the bedrock of a loving God who says that we are valued by Him. That way, no matter how much change is crashing and burning around us, we can rest in the security of a loving God who says, **"I am the Lord, I do not change"** (Malachi 3:6 NKJV). He doesn't change who He's chosen, and He doesn't change whom He loves. Wow, that's security!

#4: GOD IS FAITHFUL
"DO NOT FEAR, FOR I AM WITH YOU." (ISAIAH 43:5)

Can't you feel the joy growing inside you right now? I mean, to think God has personally chosen me brings such confidence! Beyond that, God's presence gives me strength to persevere. God's love tells me *I am valued* and allows me to feel secure.

Man, wouldn't it be great if your family were all on that same page with you? Someone has said that parents are seldom happier than their most miserable child. I hope that's not true, but I do know that people have a hard time experiencing joy as long as someone in their family is hurting.

No surprise then that right in the middle of Isaiah 43, God makes this incredible promise.

> *"Do not fear, for I am with you; I will bring your offspring from the east, and gather you from the west. I will say to north, 'Give them up!' And to the south, 'Do not hold them back.' Bring My sons from afar and My daughters from the ends of the earth, everyone who is called by My name, and whom I have created for My glory, whom I have formed, even whom I have made."* (v. 5–6)

"But you don't know how far gone my kids are. They'd never . . ." Hang on. As a pastor of a larger church, I've prayed with more parents on behalf of more rebellious kids than I can count. Let me tell you one story to build your confidence in God's faithfulness.

The first time I met Emily, she was a seriously messed-up seventeen-year-old. She and her loser friends were headed in a bad direction fast. Though her parents pleaded with her to turn her life around, she seemed bent on her own destruction. The moment she finished high school she was out the door as fast as her feet could carry her. With a pair of extra shoes and the clothes on her back, she walked away from God and her parents and moved to the far side of the world. She ended up in Sipan, this tiny island in southeast Asia. Her parents were brokenhearted. "Where is Emily tonight?" and "What is she doing?" and "Will we ever see her again?" They longed to know that their daughter was even alive. At times, they feared the worst.

One, two, five years went by—I remember a lot of prayer meetings when we called out to God for Emily. But honestly, it all seemed so hopeless. When she finally *did* phone home once or twice, she wouldn't give her number and had a whole bunch of hurtful things to say.

In Sipan, Emily got involved with a man named Kojo. He was wealthy and seductive, and lavished on her everything she thought she wanted. Together, they had a daughter.

But Emily couldn't find the peace she craved. She said, "I would walk up and down the beach with my little girl, looking for shells and beautiful things. From a human perspective I had everything, but inside I was empty." All this time her parents were persisting in prayer and asking God to bring home their daughter who, humanly speaking, seemed to have fallen off the edge of the world. Was God listening to those prayers? There were many days when the answer appeared to be a resounding *no*.

But then Emily's world collapsed. There was trouble with Kojo. She found out he was a member of the Akusa, the Japanese Mafia. At one point he was thrown into jail, but he quickly posted a million dollars cash bond to get out. She realized she had to get away, yet that tiny island became like a prison. She was terrified.

Late one night Kojo said he was coming over. As she sat on her balcony fearing a confrontation, she watched from above as he got out of his car. In that moment men poured out of the jungle around his parked car and violently grabbed him. It was the police breaking up Kojo's drug ring. Or was it God answering the prayers of Emily's parents?

Later we learned that at the very moment this was going on, her parents were praying in Chicago. Praying for God to get hold of their daughter and bring her safely home. They had no reason to keep praying, since they had seen no result, but in that moment God was doing a miracle. In the confusion of Kojo's arrest, Emily escaped to Guam and immediately called her parents. Crying and uncertain of their response, she dialed home and heard her mother say, "Emily, we love you. Come home." As soon as she could, she jumped on a plane and flew back to Chicago's O'Hare International Airport. Her parents met her at the gate, embraced her, and welcomed her and her daughter home.

> He hears the most stumbling or broken cry, the whisper, the sigh, and the requests we feel when we don't even know how to begin.

In a recent worship service, I noticed Emily as I was preaching and rejoiced in the obvious transformation God had brought to her life. Her whole appearance had changed. The anger and rebellion was gone, replaced by a joy that only comes through obedience to the Lord. As I saw her I thought of Isaiah 43 and the promise God makes about bringing our family home no matter how far gone they appear to be. It's a promise you can bank on and use to increase your faith.

Identity Point #4: I am heard.

Even when you don't feel it or see it—God hears you! He doesn't always answer how or when you want, but God does answer prayer. It's not about you saying the right words or following any silly formula. He doesn't give preference to the eloquent or to the most persuasive (as if!). The psalmist writes, **"I love the LORD, because he has heard my voice and my pleas for mercy. Because he inclined his ear to me, therefore I will call on him as long as I live"** (Psalm 116:1–2 ESV).

Are you still alive? Then keep praying. Are you interceding for someone in your family today? Maybe you too have a prodigal, a kid who wants nothing to do with God and you're praying for him or her to return. Maybe you're praying for wisdom in how to rear your toddler or for the protection of your college student across the country. Maybe you're talking to God about the future spouse of a newborn or praying to see a heart for Christ as your child enters high school. Are you calling out for the conversion of an adult child?

Keep on praying. God hears you, and He's working in ways beyond your imagination. When you do keep praying, Philippians 4:6–7 makes a huge promise.

#4 New Identity Applied: Peace

God is faithful; you are heard. Result? You have the choice to follow His program and claim His peace. Here it is in Philippians 4:6–7 (emphasis added):

> ***Be anxious for nothing, but in everything by prayer . . . let your requests be made known to God.*** *And the peace of God,* ***which surpasses all comprehension, will guard your hearts and your minds.***

Get it? Worry about nothing. Pray about everything. Expect God's peace to stand guard around your heart. Why? Because He isn't fickle about keeping His promises. A. W. Tozer says it better than I can:

> *What peace it brings to the Christian's heart to realize that our heavenly Father never differs from Himself. In coming to Him at any time we need not wonder whether we shall find Him in a receptive mood. He is always receptive to misery and need, as well as to love and faith. He does not keep office hours nor set aside periods when He will see no one. Neither does He change His mind about anything. Today, this moment, He feels toward His creatures, toward babies, toward the sick, the fallen, the sinful, exactly as He did when He sent His only begotten Son into the world to die for mankind.*

If your heart is a storm, let God hear from you, and let His faithfulness grip your heart with peace.

#5: GOD IS PATIENT
"DO NOT CALL TO MIND THE FORMER THINGS,
OR PONDER THINGS OF THE PAST." (ISAIAH 43:18)

Amazing, isn't it? Voices for personal growth and well-being in our world almost unanimously call for us to dig up our past in order to do better in the future. God says, **"Do not."**

Being gripped by God's greatness is all about today and tomorrow, not yesterday.

God is patient with you. He's not keeping tabs on how many times you fall into a certain sin. *Whoa, that's six times she's done that. One more slip-up and I'm through with her.* Do you think that what you've done shocks Him? Remember early in the chapter, God identified Himself as the One who formed you (Isaiah 43:1). He knows what you're about. Beyond that, God is prompting you to forgive and release those who have injured you so you can go forward into deeper experiences with Him. He's all about doing a new work in you today! Look at similar messages in Isaiah and Philippians:

> *"Do not call to mind the former things, or ponder things of the past. Behold, I will do something new, now it will spring forth."* (Isaiah 43:18)

> *Forgetting those things which are behind . . . reaching forward to those things which are ahead.* (Philippians 3:13 NKJV)

Put the pain and disappointment of past failures behind you and press yourself hard in the grip of this incredibly patient God.

Identity Point #5: I am forgiven.

Of course, the only reason you can forgive is because you have been forgiven. Wanna get blessed? Do what I did and read every verse in the Bible that describes God's forgiveness. In case you don't get to it soon, here are the highlights:

- *It is God's nature to forgive.* "**For You, Lord, are good, and ready to forgive, and abundant in lovingkindness to all who call upon You**" (Psalm 86:5).
- *There is no limit to God's forgiveness.* "**If** [your brother] **sins against you seven times a day, and returns to you seven times, saying, 'I repent,' forgive him**" (Luke 17:4).
- *Forgiveness was in our Lord's heart as He died on the cross.* "**But Jesus was saying, 'Father, forgive them'**" (Luke 23:34).
- *God forgives us only because Christ died to pay for our sins.* "**In** [Christ] **we have redemption through His blood, the forgiveness of sins**" (Ephesians 1:7 NKJV).
- *God is always ready to forgive us.* "**If we confess our sins, He is faithful and righteous to forgive us**" (1 John 1:9).

Every heart that truly comprehends the reality of God's forgiveness bursts forth in a fountain of praise that drenches everyone in the near vicinity.

#5 New Identity Applied: Praise

"The beasts of the field will glorify Me, the jackals and the ostriches, because I have given waters in the wilderness and rivers in the desert, to give drink to My chosen people. The people whom I formed for Myself will declare My praise." (vv. 20–21)

"I really like your hat" is not praise. Praise is more than a compliment. Praise is giving honor; it's ascribing worth to a superior. When we praise God, we express joy in His very nature and thank Him for His goodness.

When are we to praise? Right now. This minute. And at all times. We are called to bless the Lord when we see His goodness and when we don't. As my friend David Crowder sings in the song "Obsession":

Sometimes You're further than the moon, sometimes You're closer than my skin.

We are commanded to praise God in both of those circumstances.

To really be gripped by your identity in God's greatness you must wade out of the shallow waters of self-absorption into the deep waters of praising Him at all times for all things. Remember, God formed you for that very purpose. Embrace your identity as a forgiven worshiper of this all-patient God. He invites you this moment to move more deeply into whom He created you to be.

PULLING IT ALL TOGETHER

Take a deep breath, then open wide and swallow this. Or better, let these truths swallow you:

GOD'S CHARACTER	MY IDENTITY POINT	MY IDENTITY APPLIED
God is personal.	I am chosen.	Confidence
God is present.	I am strong.	Perseverance
God is loving.	I am valued.	Security
God is faithful.	I am heard.	Peace
God is patient.	I am forgiven.	Praise

It Happened to Me

LUKE

For as long as I can remember I have had a deep and abiding fear about losing one of my children to death. I know we're not supposed to find our identity in our children, and I work hard to avoid that pitfall, but it's tough. As a pastor I've stood too often with heartbroken parents at the head of tiny caskets and shared words of comfort I knew were not adequate. At least not then.

I have openly told both my church and children about the nightmares I have about my kids staying out too late and becoming road kill for some inebriated fool. It was torture to see Luke, our oldest son, drive the family car away for the first time. As I lost control of sixteen years of successful protection, I secretly feared if I lost a child I might somehow lose my faith too.

I got used to them being out on the road after a while, but for some reason simmering under the surface was a certain something I couldn't put my finger on. Even when Landon, our second son, began to drive, my fear stayed focused on Luke.

In August 2004, Luke headed off to Moody Bible Institute to prepare for pastoral ministry. I was rejoicing . . . and relieved that he was leaving his car at home. It was hard to see him go, but he was thriving and I was thrilled that we would meet up at our church camp for Labor Day weekend. He retrieved his car and picked up a friend for the 250-mile trek to the Michigan campground just north of Grand Rapids. I was already in Grand Rapids for some ministry-related meetings. Suddenly, in the middle of an afternoon meeting, I had a strong prompting in my spirit to call Luke and was a little anxious not to reach his cell phone. He's on the road and probably out of cellular range, I thought.

When the meetings ended, I jumped in my car for the final thirty miles up to Camp Harvest. As soon as I got on the road I reached for my cell phone and tried, again unsuccessfully, to contact Luke. Moments later my message notification rang, and I smiled to think he had been trying to reach me at the same time. Instead the message was from Kathy. She was only a few minutes from the camp and in a disconcerting tone asked me to call her immediately.

"Luke's been in an accident," she said (and, for a second, my heart stopped beating). "But he's OK." How do you know? What happened? Where is he? I fired off a round of questions, and she calmly gave me the number of a motorist who had seen the accident and stopped to help.

I quickly pulled over, took the number down, and dialed this Good Samaritan. Alan answered and explained that Luke's car had flipped multiple times on the freeway and landed wheels down in the ditch. No other cars were involved. Luke had apparently blown out a tire and lost control of the vehicle. The boy traveling with him was unhurt, but Luke had several cuts, and both were taken to the hospital in an ambulance.

I thanked him for his kindness, breathed a prayer of gratitude for God's mercy, and called Kathy back. I met Kathy at the exit just up the freeway, and she joined my car as we rushed back to the Grand Rapids hospital to retrieve our son . . . we thought.

We were not prepared for our first sight of Luke in the hospital. He was on a gurney behind a curtain by the counter in the emergency room. His head and chest were covered with blood, and he was crying out from the pain. He wept when he saw us—tears of sorrow, tears of grief and pain, mingled with his own expressions of thanks for God's mercy in sparing his life. Examinations revealed a number of lacerations from where his head struck the pavement through the shattered driver side window. Glass was imbedded in his skull, but the doctor felt his recovery would be full.

State police then arrived at the hospital and concurred that the SUV had rolled over at least three times, landing right-side up in the ditch. The car had burst into flames in the engine region, but others had pulled Luke from the vehicle and put out the fire.

X-rays revealed nothing of concern in the neck region, and we were greatly relieved when the doctor announced Luke's release several hours later. Though Luke was still in much pain, we were hopeful. However, when he tried to get up to leave, the throbbing in his neck became excruciating. After several exhausting and extremely hurtful attempts to rise, the doctor feared an injury the X-ray had not revealed and ordered an MRI.

Before the hour was out, the diagnosis was in: "three non-displaced fractures in C2, the second vertebra below the skull."

"He broke his neck?" we asked in shock and disbelief. "Yes," the doctor said. Normally a trauma of this sort displaces the broken bones, causing paralysis or death. C2 is the only vertebra that has an appendage the size of a small thumb extending vertically toward the base of the skull, the doctor explained. It is this "thumb" that our head rotates around, and in Luke's case it was completely severed in the accident and yet "not displaced."

"He is very lucky to be alive," the doctor told us.

Together we heard the news that Luke would have to wear a halo device for eight to twelve weeks and see a specialist in Chicago about further surgery. Kathy and I huddled in grateful prayer around our firstborn son, still in so much pain, still covered in blood, and we worshiped the Lord for mercy shown and undeserved. In a few minutes they asked us to leave as they lightly sedated our son and drilled four holes in his skull to attach the device that would keep his neck immobilized for the next three months. It was almost 2:00 a.m. when we left him at the hospital and drove in grateful silence to the camp.

We awoke early to a flood of caring contacts from those who love our family. By God's grace, Luke was released for an ambulance ride to Chicago on Labor Day, and within a week he was sleeping well and gaining strength. As the son of a radio preacher he had hoped for some anonymity at Moody, but it was not to be. His halo made him a little hard to miss as *he commuted to campus, and a supportive, praying student body continually encouraged him.*

Our first visit to the doctor produced another MRI and the fear that if the bones shifted without healing in this area with such limited blood supply, a surgery would be necessary to screw the broken pieces back together. It was a very tough autumn. Luke slept on our recliner for fifteen weeks, and the halo did not come off until December 15. But the Lord gave him grace and was clearly shaping his character with a full-size chisel.

Through diligence and perseverance and in spite of pain, Luke completed his semester at school, and much more importantly, we deeply believe, God spared our son. We all learned a lot—some of which is still too tender to talk about. What I can tell you is that worship has reached a new volume in each of us.

Luke is a gifted worship leader and youth leader in our church. He loves to sing and lead others in praise, and someday he wants to preach. Those are commitments between Luke and his Lord, and by God's grace I don't ever want to get caught "between the hammer and the work."

If God had sovereignly chosen to allow our son to suffer, who am I to say no? Just a fraction of further pressure or an increment of movement on Luke's neck, or if the car had landed upside down, or if the first car to come along had not extinguished the fire, or if the neck bones had splintered as Luke was pulled from the wreck, or . . . and our son would be with the Lord. I have thought and prayed often over these past few months, wondering if I would have passed the test of faithfulness had the Lord chosen to take our first son home. I know firsthand how essential it is that we base all of our identity in the Lord Himself. I know this because . . . it happened to me.

So What About You?

Let's make sure we learn that lesson by faith. I know, dear friends, having experienced it, how hard this can be. God has always been proven faithful, but I would not wish that on anyone. Let's scour the landscape of our life and search out any point of identity not rooted in God Himself. Let's make very sure that God reigns supreme over this matter of our identity so that if in His sovereignty He allows such a profound loss to penetrate our perfect worlds, we will not have to race to this place but will, in fact, have the strength of already being there. May God protect us from so loving our children (or our ministries, or our careers or our spouses) that they become our identity instead of our relationship with Him.

My prayer for you and me is, *Lord, allow us to love without adoring. Teach us to be involved with our loved ones but never idolizing, and grant that they never find themselves in the place of Isaac. Lest again You step in "to save both father and son from the consequences of an uncleansed love."*[1] *Teach us ever more deeply what it means to find our identity in You and in You to **"live and move and have our being"*** (Acts 17:28 ESV).

LET'S PRAY

Lord,

Thank You for the freedom I find in the truth of Your Word. I acknowledge before You in this moment of honesty that too often I have taken my identity from thinking, *I'm successful in this business thing*, or *I'm a great dad*, or *Look at my garden or my lawn*. Lord, how ridiculous. Please forgive me.

Let my only source of truth of who I am be You. Thank You for who *You* are. The truth about You eclipses everything. Thank You for Your love and Your faithfulness. Thank You for being personally present in my life. Help me live in light of that truth every day as I lift my voice to You in praise and in gratitude for Your amazing love.

You are my Rock and my Redeemer, and I rest in You.

—*Amen.*

MAKE IT PERSONAL

1. Don't Listen to the Enemy.

    It is a powerful thing to walk through this life with a firm confidence in your identity . . . as God knows you. But I want to alert you to our enemy, Satan, who is trying to mess you up about who you really are. If he can confuse you, he can accomplish a lot in your life.

    If you've not yet committed your life to Jesus Christ, I need to talk very candidly. Satan is lying to you. He's telling you that you're OK just as you are. "You don't need Jesus. You're a pretty good person —God should accept you into heaven just as you are. You're ready to meet God." *That is a lie*—you are not ready to meet God. If you die today, you will stand before a righteous, holy God, and He will say, **"I never knew you"** (Matthew 7:23).

    You are not ready to meet God unless you have submitted your life to Jesus Christ. Please, today get this matter settled.

    Now, if you know Christ, you need to know that Satan invests a lot of energy trying to get you to live apart from who you really are. He wants you to remember your failures. He wants you to live in discouragement and defeat. He wants to tuck those things in your pocket so he can throw them up in your face every time you try to take a step forward with God. He says, "You're a loser. You flunked out big time. God's not very fired up about you anymore." Everything Satan says to you is bent on your defeat and your ineffectiveness as a representative of Christ. He hates you because he hates Jesus Christ. Instead of letting those cancers grow, go back to what God says about you. Rehearse the list of the five things we talked about in this chapter and how they define who you are and how you should live. Either photocopy or rewrite the grid on page 166 and put it somewhere you're going to see it through the day. Instead of pumping yourself up with cotton candy phrases, return to what God's Word says about you.

    The truth is: God is fired up about you.

2. Look at the cool stuff God says about you. Personalize these truths about your true identity by filling in the blanks *with your own name:*

> In 1 Corinthians 6:20, God says that _____ has been bought with a price and that _____ belongs to almighty God.

> Ephesians 1:5 says _____ has been adopted as God's child.

> Colossians 2:13 says _____ has been redeemed and forgiven of all _____'s sins.

> Romans 8:1 says there is no condemnation to _____ because _____ is in Christ.

> Romans 8:28 says _____ can be assured that "all things work together" for _____'s good.

> Romans 8:38 says _____ cannot be separated from the love of God.

> Philippians 3:20 says _____ is a citizen of heaven.

> Hebrews 4:16 says _____ can find grace and mercy in time of need.

> In Matthew 5:13–14, Jesus says _____ is the salt of the earth. _____ is the light of the world.

> First Corinthians 3:16 says _____ is God's "temple."

> Ephesians 2:10 says _____ is God's workmanship.

> Philippians 4:13 says that today, _____ can do all things through Christ who strengthens _____.

3. How does what you've read and learned in this chapter affect your prayer life? How does your true identity make prayer:

> More of a relationship and less of a performance?
>
> More of a life attitude and less of an observance?
>
> More an expression of worship and less of a grocery check-off list?

Thank God right now for the realities revealed in this chapter about your true identity. Ask Him to root them deep into your heart and prevent the enemy of your soul from stealing this seed of truth from you. Praise Him for His faithfulness to you in all times and in all places.

HOW TO STAY GRIPPED by the GREATNESS of GOD

I'VE SAID IT FOR YEARS: The Christian life is both a crisis and a process. It begins in a crisis called conversion and continues through a process called sanctification.

Sanctification is the process by which God takes His forgiven children and transforms them daily into the image of Christ. Second Corinthians 3:18 describes it: **"But we all, with unveiled face, beholding as in a mirror the glory of the Lord, are being transformed into the same image from glory to glory, just as from the Lord."**

Throughout the process of transformation there is a continual cycle of crisis and process. My sinful heart wanders lazily from the grace of God, and He graciously uses the crisis of some painful circumstance to bring me back. At other times I stubbornly refuse to be changed in a particular area, and God's abundant goodness brings me to my knees. (**"Or do you think lightly of the riches of His kindness and tolerance and patience, not knowing that the kindness of God leads you to repentance?"** [Romans 2:4].)

Each of these crisis points could easily be described as a time when God gripped me afresh with His greatness. Like the hymn writer said, "Prone to wander, Lord, I feel it, prone to leave the God I love."[1] And because of our wandering hearts, we should be so immensely grateful that God continuously reaches out and takes hold of us again.

Do you know God's greatness firsthand?

Do you long to *stay* within the joyful confines of His glorious grip? I suspect your answer, like mine, is a resounding *yes!* Here's what you need to do . . .

First, ask yourself, "Have I even had a pivotal point in my life when I turned from self to God alone?" You've just about finished reading all about the greatness of God, but if you've never turned to Him in humble repentance and faith, you can't come close to understanding what we've been talking about.

Does that make sense to you? If you're not 100 percent sure, why not choose right now? Your story can be: "I was reading this book on God and figured out that I had never chosen to know Him personally. I knew things about Him, but I didn't know Him intimately. I hit a crisis point where I needed to make a decision. So I chose to repent of my sin. I told God how sorry I was, and I thanked Him for sending His Son Jesus to pay for my sin. I invited Christ to come into my life, to forgive me and begin a new work (a process) of transformation in me." If you want to make that decision, you may pray a prayer like this from your heart. Yes! Right now.

> *Lord,*
>
> I know that I am a sinner and that on my own I am not prepared to meet God. I believe that Jesus died to pay the penalty for my sin. I believe that He rose from the dead. Right now in this moment I turn from my sin and I embrace Jesus Christ by faith. Come into my life and forgive my sins. Change me. Make me the man or woman that You want me to be. I give my life to You today.
>
> I pray in Jesus' name,
>
> *—Amen.*

OK, believer in Christ Jesus, how about you? How long since you've been deeply affected by just how awesome and great our God really is? Do you want that again more than anything?

God calls even the most faithful Christian to times of struggle so that He can give you a new and transforming glimpse of His greatness. Perhaps you picked up this book during the very kind of crisis we are talking about. You hoped to get some spiritual survival help during really hard times.

Or maybe you're in a time of victory. God has given you some huge success. His goodness and grace has so overwhelmed you that you want to put some words of worship to how you are feeling.

God is using all of these circumstances—good and difficult—to draw You closer to Himself.

> **W**hen was the last time God got a grip on your life?

Best of all are God's surprises. You're going along in your routine and—wham!—right out of the blue, you sense His awesomeness on some random day. And your world is rocked, and you're taken to your knees.

And sometimes when you should be on your knees you're running your own program instead. Standing at that fork in the road, you must decide to obey or rebel, and God in His grace makes you aware of His greatness.

Do you relate to any of these situations? At one time or another, I think all of us who know and love the Lord have met with Him in these kinds of ways.

But that's not where you can live the Christian life long term. Those mountaintop experiences may be the fuel for our joy and victory, but that enthusiasm of being gripped by God must inevitably fade into disciplined, purposeful obedience. However, even in the routine we can sense the abiding presence of God upon us. Being gripped by God's greatness can emerge daily in the context of seeking Him through His Word and in prayer. You can't expect God to show up in dramatic ways if you don't show up before Him in faithful, consistent ways. That means submitting to Him in three specific, personal areas: our minds, our emotions, and our wills.

BEING GRIPPED BY THE GREATNESS OF GOD INVOLVES MY MIND

When God reveals Himself in some fresh way, my focus is on Him, not myself. The time is meant to give me a fresh awareness of His reality and nearness.

Being gripped by God means I don't stay in spiritual kindergarten all my life. I grow in my knowledge of God and His Word. For the believers at Colossae, the apostle Paul prayed for their minds to be gripped by God's greatness: **"that you may be filled with the knowledge of His will in all spiritual wisdom and understanding, so that you will walk in a manner worthy of the Lord, to please Him in all respects, bearing fruit in every good work and increasing in the knowledge of God"** (Colossians 1:9–10).

BEING GRIPPED BY THE GREATNESS OF GOD INVOLVES MY EMOTIONS

When God gets a grip on my life, I *do* feel something. In Scripture, every time someone has a genuine encounter with God, the person is on his or her face before Him. When God shows us a fraction of His glory, our response is fear—a humble, holy reverence of Him. It's like a veil drops from my eyes, and I gasp at how great, and how close, and how real He is.

We've come too far in our study to entertain some cotton-candy, feel-good-at-all-cost attitude toward God. I know you don't want that. You want to be in right relationship with Him. You know already, but let me reiterate: You can't afford to be in a wrong place with God. Don't allow some particular sin to exist in your life for days, weeks, or months. As a follower of Jesus Christ, don't go to bed at night without getting things right with God. Salvation may have taken the fear of hell away, but never let it take away your holy fear of being in true connectedness with the living God.

BEING GRIPPED BY THE GREATNESS OF GOD
INVOLVES MY WILL

God is not simply about giving His children goose bumps. I don't long for the dramatic—I long for the unmistakable, the genuine unveiling of the glory of God. And when He does get a grip on me, it's so I would *do* something differently. So that I would forever be changed, impacted not only in what I know and what I feel, but also in what I do.

Probably the clearest indication that God has gripped your heart is a heightened reverence and respect for His Word. How much power does God's Word have over your life? Can God's Word change your opinion on a subject? Are you done treating God's Word like a salad bar—some of this and a little of that and *no, none of that*? God says, **"To this one I will look, to him who is humble and contrite of spirit, and who trembles at My Word"** (Isaiah 66:2). Do you tremble at God's Word? Does your will spring into action at every command of the Lord? These are the disciplines of remaining firmly in His grip. To do otherwise is to fight and squirm free. He will not hold you against your will. But really, where would you rather be?

Being gripped by God means no more reminiscence of when your faith was vibrant, but instead offering yourself moment by moment—mind, emotions, and will—to the thrilling discovery of the greatness of God. Immersing yourself in His mysterious, unsearchable, indescribable character.

Well, the information is on the table about who God is, who you are, and what He will do for you when you embrace those two realities.

Will you do it?

LET'S PRAY

Great God,
    Your greatness is elevated in my eyes. You are high and lifted up, and Your glory fills the whole earth. I delight myself in You. I do not shrink back from seeking Your face but place myself in the stream of Your ever-flowing grace. And seeing here just a glimpse of Your greatness, I refuse to substitute emotionalism for what is genuine

and biblical and true. I want the real thing. I want to spend my life discovering Your greatness in rich, fulfilling ways. **"You will make known to me the path of life; in Your presence is fullness of joy; in Your right hand there are pleasures forever"** (Psalm 16:11).

—Amen.

NOTES

Chapter 1: Gripped by the Holiness of God

1. Reginald Heber, "Holy, Holy, Holy." In public domain.

Chapter 6: Gripped by My Identity in God

1. A. W. Tozer, *The Pursuit of God*.

Epilogue: How to Stay Gripped by the Greatness of God

1. Robert Robinson, "Come, Thou Fount." In public domain.

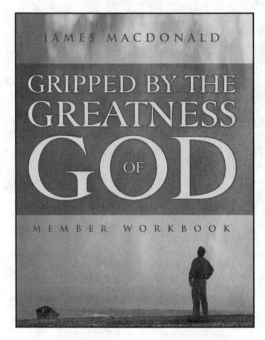

God's power can
transform your life!

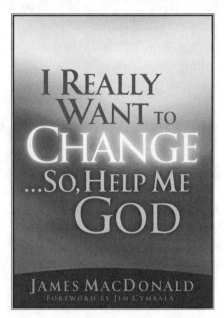

Change is never easy. Sometimes it's downright painful. But because we are called as believers in Christ to holiness, we simply can't stay as we are. This is a book about how to achieve a different you. It includes study questions, exercises, and prayers that lead to change.

This is the ideal book for people who are serious about seeing lasting changes take place in their character and conduct. The author is both compassionate and confrontational—no kid gloves! You will either read it through and honestly put it into practice or you will invent another excuse for staying as you are!

—Warren Wiersbe, author and speaker

This book gets to the heart of what needs to take place if we are going to really see genuine and lasting change in our lives. I highly recommend both James's ministry and his powerful book to you.

—Greg Laurie, pastor, Harvest Christian Fellowship

I Really Want to Change...So, Help Me God   ISBN: 0-8024-3423-1

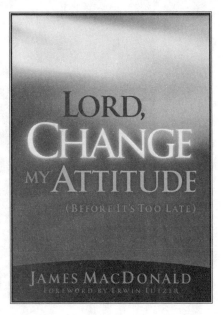
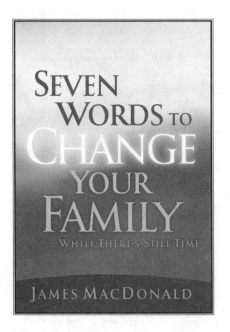

Gripped By the Greatness of God Team

Acquiring Editor
Greg Thornton

Back Cover Copy
Michele Straubel

Copy Editor
Jim Vincent

Cover Design
David Riley & Associates

Interior Design
BlueFrog Design

Printing and Binding
Dickinson Press Inc.
Dekker Bookbinding-Cloth Binding

The typeface for the text of this book is
Berkeley